THIS IS WHAT SUCCESS LOOKS LIKE

13 Steps Anyone Can Follow

THIS IS WHAT SUCCESS LOOKS LIKE: 13 Steps Anyone Can Follow
Copyright © 2014 Bryan Zimmerman

Cover Design: Chris Cruz
Interior Layout: Zanna Jezek

Printed in the U.S.A.
10 9 8 7 6 5 4 3 2 1

Library of Congress Cataloging-in-Publication Data
Zimmerman, Bryan 1977 -

Library of Congress Control Number: 2014914186
Distinct Press, St. Petersburg, Florida

ISBN-10: 099160895X
ISBN-13: 978-0-9916089-5-9

Summary: Successful author, business owner and online entrepreneur, Bryan Zimmerman, teaches you 13 steps that will catapult you to success in any industry you choose.

1. Internet Marketing 2. Business Development 3. Working from Home 4. Make Money Online 5. Personal Development 6. Marketing

Distinct Press
6822 22nd Avenue N., Suite 345
Saint Petersburg, Florida 33710-3918

For more information on our books, please visit: www.DistinctPress.com
For more information on the author, please visit: www.BryanZimmermansBlog.com

THIS IS WHAT
SUCCESS LOOKS LIKE

13 Steps Anyone Can Follow

Bryan Zimmerman

A DISTINCT PRESS BOOK
U.S.A.

*To all those who have lived the grind that success takes,
remember those who are still climbing.
Never forget that we all started somewhere
and in the end we'll all be equal again.
It's the journey that defines who we are
and the legacy we leave behind.
To anyone who is not afraid to put themselves
on the line for a chance at a better life
than what you've been handed,
I salute you.
Life is short, so live each day
as if it's the last chance you get to leave an impression.
Play hard and I'll see you on the other side.*

CONTENTS

Introduction

You've done it already and you don't even realize it. You most likely picked up this book because of the differences in what the title says and what the picture portrays and even while you're reading this first paragraph, you already have a pre-conceived notion of who I am. Don't feel bad about it though, I did it on purpose. What you may not realize however, the act of having a preset opinion or conclusion about someone or something is one of the biggest reasons people leave so much on the table when it comes to success.

The majority of people seem to think successful people act a certain way or they have a certain look, the suit, neat haircut, clean appearance and over all body language. All things that tend to give off the impression that a person presenting these things is successful. While a person such as myself, who has multiple tattoos, long hair, who loves to wear tee shirts and jeans is someone who either has no motivation or still thinks they're twenty years old. Again, a misjudgment that can cost people tremendous amounts of money.

The fact is, you couldn't pay me to wear a suit. You couldn't pay me to follow the rat race and conform to what the so called "leaders" in the business world say just so they can march another ant into their army. You couldn't pay me to go to a fancy party just to hob nob with a bunch of people that are faker than a thousand dollar bill. Why? Because it gets you nowhere!

You see, what I will do is walk into that fancy party dressed a lot more casual than anyone else and I do it on purpose. Just as you picked up this book because of the cover and title differences, I want to see people's true reactions. I want to see it all, their glares, their smirks, their uncomfortableness, and their process of creating a preconceived opinion of who I am. Then to have a little fun with it, I'll walk up to one of them and start up a conversation. Many times you can see not only the uncertainty in their eyes, but the fear of others around them watching how they react. It's great, and I love every minute of it, but there's also a very distinct purpose behind it. I'm looking for those who recognize there's something different there.

What usually happens is once those who were at first stand offish find out what it is I do, their whole demeanor changes. Now it's okay, I have a bunch of tattoos and am wearing a tee shirt at their party. Why the change all of a sudden? Because they know that I have the ability to help further their own goals, financial situations, connections and more. Here's the key though, I already know as much about them as I need to from their initial reactions. So while they now suddenly have an interest, I do not. I'm now networking with those who recognized the situation from the start and thought there's more to this situation than what it looks like. In this book, I'm going to teach you all about this, and so much more.

Here's the facts. Society and the so called "leaders" of it, have brainwashed the majority of people into following a pattern of how success can be achieved. I'm going to smash that to pieces in this book because what has/is being taught is bullshit.

Society would lead you to believe that you need to go to school, get a degree, find a job, bust your ass and you can retire when you're 60 with a pension. They teach you to save your money along the way and then you can live out your golden years comfortably. Now let's look at the reality of it and get to the truth.

The economy in the last five to ten years has proved that nobody is safe in today's business world unless you own something. Think about all of the people who lost their jobs, jobs they'd worked at for ten, twenty years that were all of a sudden let go. They followed the "blueprint" and were well on their way until the ball dropped on them like a hammer. Overnight, their pensions and their careers were gone. They had zero control over the situation and if you've been there, you know it's not pleasant. How were they going to pay their bills, feed their families and all the other things that happen when your income just gets cut off? The sin in those situations? Their life was controlled by strings that weren't attached to their own hands!

You're probably thinking that even if you own a business, that doesn't give you a safety net that saves you. You're right, but you just made a mistake so many others make. Your way of thinking needs to be changed immediately! Sure, it's not fail safe, but it's in your hands now and that gives you a hell of a lot better chance at it than if your life hangs in the balance of someone else's business.

Here's what most people won't tell you because they know people like the "feel good" vibe it creates when it's said that anyone can do it. Well, not anyone can do it. Everyone is capable of doing it, but that doesn't mean they can or will. The truth is, everyone likes the idea of being successful, but only a small percentage of people are willing to do what it takes to make it more than just an idea. The rest are sentenced to a life of marching in line with the rest of the ants, working to make someone else a shit load of money. I'm not sugarcoating anything, that's not my style.

Think about this for a moment though. I have a total of two weeks of college. I worked as a waiter and bartender for 8 years. I did hard labor construction work for 10 years. None of these things are rocket science and none of them take any real education. Yet, I also I built an online business that at the time of this writing has processed over 70 million dollars.

There's thousands of books that teach you "how to" build businesses online or off. What this book is going to show you is the insight and exact formula I used and perfected to get to the top of every single job I've ever had. That's right, I reached the exact position I wanted to in every job I have ever taken with what I'm about to teach you. While others want to give you generalized "steps", I'm going to teach you angles, triggers and plans that bring results.

My real qualification to lead you on this journey? I don't forget where I came from, it's that simple. I still relate better to people who have less than people who have it all. I like the honesty of someone who's hungry for success versus the "look at me" show it becomes when you're in a group of people who have money. I don't like the fact people think because of their status they're better than others. I wasn't born into privilege and I've busted my ass for everything I have. Yes, my company has processed millions online, but when I started out, I had no idea how to send an email. I've been a complete rookie in everything I've done, but I've always come out on top and I've always used the same formula I'm about to share with you.

Let's get this grammar and punctuation part out of the way as well. I'm no English Major and I write like I talk. If you need to read something that's perfectly formatted and punctuated, then you better put this book down now. Do me a favor and punch yourself in the stomach after you set it down. If you're looking at grammar and punctuation more than what the words you're about to read say, then you will probably wind up working for someone like me. You know what it meant or what it was supposed to say. Get down off your high horse and deal with it.

As you turn the page to Chapter 1, I ask you to forget about every idea of how success is supposed to happen. Forget society's rules, forget preconceived notions, and forget previous ideas and thoughts on success. Open your mind and put yourself in the present. Remind yourself that right now, this very moment as you read this, this is as old as you've ever been and the youngest you will ever be again. There is no time to waste. You've let success wait on you long enough....

Chapter 1

Prepping The Slate

Most people only read the first fifteen pages of a book. If you're smart, you'll read every page in this one. But due to human nature, I wanted to put the most powerful content, the information that can help you immediately, right at the front of the book. The formula I'm going to teach you can be broken down into thirteen steps. Some of these are going to require you to do a bit of thinking on your part, but don't worry, none of them are difficult. Within these thirteen steps, I'm not only going to break them down and explain them, I'm also going to give you examples that actually happened to me so you can see them in real world settings. At the end of the thirteen steps, I give you a blueprint to follow that will help you tremendously in getting these thirteen steps to work best for you.

While I will talk about mindset some, there will be none of that "touch your heart and tell yourself you're going to be a millionaire" garbage. While *The Secret* is an extremely popular piece of information, in my opinion, it's bullshit. Actions get people what they want, not repeating "magic" words to yourself. I've never seen anyone get rich by telling themselves they deserve to be rich. If that worked, the entire nation would be millionaires instead of having a massive unemployment rate. Actions make you successful, not words.

Take your time going through these as well. Rome wasn't built in a day and neither are successful businesses or situations. These days, the way advertisement is done, especially with online businesses, everything seems like it can happen immediately. Put that out of your mind, it will only effect the process and yield the opposite of the results you want. Building it takes time and strategic planning, but the juice is worth the squeeze, trust me.

I highly suggest you take out a notebook and write things down as you read through this. Yes, you can go through and highlight things, but there is no better way to do it than to write something down when it strikes you as important. This way you can go right to your notebook and see the most important things you wrote down. This is a huge time saver and prevents you from thumbing back through, looking for that one part or sentence amongst all the others you may highlight. Also, you will definitely need a notebook when we get into the blueprint chapters and writing things down ahead of time will make that section much easier for you to create.

Finally, go somewhere that you won't be bothered while you're reading and writing. The flow of concentration is going to be very strong as you get into this. The last thing you want is to be in the zone and really focused, only to be interrupted. Give the people around you instructions not to bother you unless it's an emergency.

This is the beginning of your success, the foundation, so to speak. You can't expect to build a proper foundation, one that you will build a legacy on, if you aren't 100% focused. Once you have the above in place, let's begin with the first step.

Chapter 2

The Conversation

I titled this chapter "The Conversation" because that's exactly what's going to happen in step one. You're going to have a conversation with yourself. Depending on what your situation in your life currently is and what it is you that want, will determine the content of that conversation.

For me, this conversation has happened twice and they both had major impacts on my life and success. Many things you will read in this book are things I've never told anyone. Not that I'm ashamed of any of them, but because I've never thought about the outcomes of those decisions and the effects it had on my life before I sat down to write this. As I was thinking about my formula, I realized just how vital this first step is and how things would have been different had I not done it.

This first step, while simple in instruction, may be the hardest of them all because it requires you to be completely honest with yourself. You see, humans are very good at lying to each other. It happens all of the time and no matter how big or small that lie is, you yourself know when you're not being honest. The other person may never know, but you know it. You cannot lie to yourself, you just can't do it. You know damn good and well when you're trying to convince yourself of something that you know isn't true, it just doesn't work.

For the first step, get away from everything that is a distraction. Any noise that can break your concentration, any people that can make you lose focus and just be by yourself. If that happens after everyone goes to bed, fine. If you have to go sit in your car in a parking lot to make it happen, then that's what you have to do. Find a place you can be alone with yourself for this. It's extremely important.

Here is where you put away all of the walls you have built. There are no emotions here. It is as if you are completely alone on an island with nobody to criticize your thoughts, ideas or decisions. All of the "why can't I", "if I only could", "I can't handle it" and any other "can't" phrases go away here. It's at this point you want to look inward and you ask yourself –

"What is it I really want and what am I willing to do to get it?"

It's very important here that you ask yourself and yourself only this question. Remember, your spouse, friends, kids, negativity and everything else that goes in your daily life doesn't exist here. This is your chance to search for the answer without any outside distractions. Spend some time with it, it's most likely not something that you'll be able to answer in a split second.

The first time I had this conversation with myself, I was nineteen years old. While I was having a great time living a care-free life that many nineteen year olds do, one afternoon it just hit me. To this day, I can still remember the moment as if it was hours ago. I lived in a fraternity house with ten other guys at the time and as an afternoon ritual, we would all meet in the garage and pass a few joints around.

About an hour into hanging out in the garage, for some reason we all started talking about what it was we wanted to do. I listened to one guy talk about how he wanted to be a doctor, another about how he wanted to be a veterinarian and another how he wanted to be a lawyer. I was listening to them talk with such passion and determination, the way anyone usually talks about something they want.

It was at that point I suddenly took another look around the room and began to put an age on each one of them. Twenty-six, twenty-four, twenty-seven and another at twenty-three. None of them were close to graduating for at least another couple of years, and yet here they were, talking about the things they wanted to become.

Now anyone who knows anything about some of those professions also knows it takes more than just a regular college degree. You have to have good grades, then you have to attend another four to five years of specialized school before you can be ready to enter the work field in that profession. These guys didn't have a prayer in hell of ever accomplishing that before they were pushing forty, yet they were down in the garage, getting high with no signs of putting any effort towards it.

That split second it took to analyze that changed my life. I got up, made up an excuse I had something to do and went to my room and locked the door. I knew the house would clear out in twenty minutes, so I waited for them to leave. I then had the conversation with myself.

Did I want to be the one down in that room at twenty-three

11

years old, talking about what I wanted to do? Hell no. I knew that was a quick road to nowhere. I knew I had to make a change, and at that time I wanted to play professional golf. So I asked myself what I was willing to give up to make that happen.

Did I think about what my friends, my brothers were going to think? Absolutely. But I did that before I had the conversation with myself. I knew they were going to be disappointed I was leaving. I knew all the fun I would be missing out on, the parties, sorority girls, clubs and everything else that goes along with college life. I put all that away and it came down to that important question.

"What is it I really want and what am I willing to do to get it?"

My answer was simple… All of it!

Within days, I had plans set and I was ready to go. I was moving to Florida and I had even set a date when I was leaving.

This is the point when fear catches many people. The fear of the unknown, of what can happen, of what will happen and how will things be different. There's a great line in the movie *After Earth* that talks about fear. In it, the guy played by Will Smith is talking to his son and tells him:

"Fear is not real. It is a product of thoughts you create. Do not misunderstand me. Danger is very real. But fear is a choice."

Obviously at nineteen, there's not much to fear with change, but the second time I had the conversation came at a much different point in my life.

While I did play golf professionally for a time, it was never at a level that made much money, other than hustling (and that's another book all together). I was thirty-three years old, I had been working construction for almost nine years, I was married and I had three kids.

Anyone who has done construction knows it's a grueling job. You're up at sunrise, home at dark most times, and you're damn tired when you get there. Even though I had worked my way to the top of the corporation, the work load was just as rough.

My wife had just had twins about three months earlier, and needless to say, sleep was nonexistent. While I was making decent money, the strain of being gone all the time, being tired constantly and the stress of new born twins, my family life was falling apart.

I wanted more out of life than being gone all day breaking my back. I wanted to not be a stranger to my kids as I only saw them for minutes a day or sometimes not until the weekend. I saw so little of my first daughter the first two years of her life, she actually told me to go away and go back to work a few times when I came home. Hard to deal with, to say the least.

One day it happened again. I was sitting at the dinner table frustrated at how the days and weeks had been going. My wife was angry with me for not doing something, the twins were crying and my oldest daughter was fighting for attention. I thought to myself "is this all there is? Is this what it's going to be like? Something's got to change, what's going on right now isn't going to work."

That night I waited for everyone to go to sleep. I got out of bed and sat on the couch. I put the sound of the kids crying, the thought of the wife being angry, job, the house and everything else that could alter my decision aside and I asked myself again.

"What is it I really want and what am I willing to do to get it?"

Once again, the answer was simple. All of it, but including my family.

Were there concerns? If there were, they weren't on my end. I had a house to pay for, I had mouths to feed and I had bills to pay, but I didn't care. I'd collect aluminum cans on the side of the road if I had to, to make ends meet, but the current situation was going to change. I had been dabbling in online marketing for a couple of years and while I was making some money, it wasn't anywhere near what I was making in construction. All I knew was that I wanted more and I had to do what I had to do to get it.

A week later, I gave my notice at the construction company. Within a year, I had doubled what I was making in construction, online. In the three years after the first, I've multiplied it ten times over.

Now I can play with my kids anytime I want. I can go play golf anytime I want. I can pretty much do whatever I want whenever I want. It didn't happen overnight, but it all started with this first step. Without it, I very well may still be sitting in that garage talking about what I want instead of doing it. That's the REAL dream, is it not? To have the ability to do whatever you want, whenever you want. It's there, and it's there for everyone.

I'll show you exactly how I did it within the remaining steps, but this first step is really the most important one. If you don't have a clear idea of what it is you want, stay with step one until you do. Your conclusion now becomes your goal. If you try and move on before, your results will not be what you want.

In step two, I'll show you how to map out exactly how to get to what you decided in step one.

Chapter 3

The Treasure Map

When you think about treasure maps, immediately you think of pirates, gold filled chests, "X marks the spot" and images of people daring enough to go against the grain. Pirates lived their lives on their own terms and as you've now got a clear understanding of what you want, you will begin to live on your own terms as well.

While the thought of finding a treasure map sounds great, you're about to create something even better. A map of how you're going to reach the goal you decided on in the first step, *The Conversation*. I'm going to assume you've decided on what you're willing to give up to make this goal a reality, but there is one huge piece that is missing.

I'm not sure whose line this is, but I love it and it's 100% accurate.

"A goal without a plan is not a goal at all. It's a wish"

It's one thing to decide on a goal, be focused on it, shout it out to the world for accountability and go gung-ho after it, but if you don't actually map it out, you're going to fail.

You hear all of the big name "self-help" guru's talk about how important goal setting is and how if you don't do it, you're just setting yourself up for failure. This is partially true, but what seems to always get left out is the fact you can't just write a bunch of goals down on a piece of paper, tape them to your wall and expect to reach them.

The most important thing is that you must also write down HOW your plan to reach them!

It does you no good to set a goal of being financially secure but then having no plan behind it on how you're going to achieve it. You have to strategize it, formulate it and map it out, step by step. You wouldn't get a two-thousand piece puzzle, dump it on the table and just proceed to try and put random pieces together. You'd formulate a plan for it. You would start by putting the edges together, then you would separate things into like colors. It's likely you would work on one section of those colors at a time, and then blend them together as the picture on the box shows.

As you complete each part or your puzzle, you gain a sense of accomplishment. With each accomplishment, you gain confidence in the direction you are taking. Not only can you see it, but you can also feel the progress you're making on what will very soon become a finished puzzle.

This is how you will now expand on that initial goal you set. You will build your treasure map which will guide you to your goal. Each piece will be like a piece of your puzzle and as you continue to put the pieces together, not only does your confidence and progress grow, but you are watching yourself get closer and closer to your ultimate goal.

The beauty of this method is that your life will change well before you reach your ultimate goal. Each day you're going to accomplish something that brings you one step closer. This keeps you focused on the now and not on all of the things that have to happen first before you get there.

So how exactly do we expand on what we decided in step one? We break it all the way down into much smaller goals. Then we take those, and we break them down again and again. Since I don't know what you have chosen, we'll look at a couple of examples from my treasure maps, taken right from the notebooks I wrote them in.

Remember, I told you I reached the position I wanted to in every job I've ever taken, so no matter what you chose as your goal, this formula applies.

If you've ever worked at a restaurant as a server, you know there are certain sets of table stations that make more money than others. You also know that those stations are usually given to the servers who have been there the longest and are the best at their jobs. Along with those stations come much earlier times to get cut and get to leave for the night, than other stations.

When I first began waiting tables, I wanted one of those "good money, and go home early" stations, and I wanted it quickly. In order to do this, I had to structure out what it would take to basically force them to put me in one.

The first thing I did was watch how everyone else acted, responded and adjusted during a shift. I'll cover this much deeper later in another step, but I had to figure out exactly what it was going to take to give me the best chance to get the station I wanted. Once I had a good idea, I wrote out my plan.

On the following page is a direct excerpt from it and I want you to notice how detailed it is.

Good Money – Go Home Early Plan

1. Be ready for work thirty minutes before time to leave.
2. Get to work no later than fifteen minutes early.
3. Say "hello" to everyone I see as I enter the building and make sure to USE THEIR NAMES.
4. Find managers and/or owner and say "hello" before starting the shift.
5. Ask the cooks and dish crew if they need any drinks.
6. Say "hello" to bus boys and ask them how they're doing.
7. Help the hostesses with the drinks, their tables and customers.
8. Run food no less than ten times for other people.
9. Grab plates under manager's window and take to dish pit no less than five times.
10. Pre-bus table down to needing to be wiped only at least six times.
11. Check with bartenders to see if they need anything at least three times.
12. Check with cooks and dish crew near the end of shift to see if they need drinks.
13. Ask the managers if there is anything they need me to do before ending the shift and clocking out.
14. Say "thank you" and "good bye" to all of the back of house staff before leaving, remembering to USE THEIR NAMES.
15. Say "thank you" to bus boys, bartenders, hostesses and managers before leaving, remembering to USE THEIR NAMES.
16. Double check that all of my tables and side work is done and complete before leaving.

These are sixteen things on a list that I wrote down which literally gave me an exact blueprint on what I needed to do to not only get the attention of the managers, but also get me in the good graces of the cooks, dishwashers, bus boys, bartenders and hostesses. You also notice I didn't mention one thing about MY job and what I had to do as far as serving the tables I had in my current station.

Also, I want you to notice the detail in the list. I used actual numbers of times to do things instead of a general statement. This is extremely important! If someone says I'll do it sometime tomorrow, they're a hundred times more likely to not do it than if they say "I'll do it at 5:00 p.m. tomorrow".

I not only wrote down to say "hello" to everyone, I also put to remember to use their names, in all capital letters. It is the little details like this that make all the difference.

Now, let's break that list down even further and fully understand why those things were so important in getting the station I wanted to get. You'll also get a much better understanding of how small goals like this turn into the success of reaching the bigger goals that you set. Remember, there is nothing in that list that talks about what my actual job of serving my tables entailed.

NUMBERS ONE AND TWO on the list go hand in hand and basically make sure I am EARLY to work. There is nothing that will get you put in the dog house faster than being late, so by setting a goal that I am ready thirty minutes before I leave, ensures that I will be there at least fifteen minutes before my shift starts. It also ensures I have time to do number three without interfering with starting my actual shift.

Now, this obviously relates to actually having a job and showing up to it, but when you work for yourself on the internet and have no set schedule, it's even more important! One of the first things I figured out when I started working online was there was no "clock" to punch in and out. There was no one standing over my shoulder to yell at me if I wasn't starting to work on time. I had to SET a time I was going to start and I had to WRITE it down! This became my "clock in" time and I treated it the same way I would as if I had to be somewhere.

Granted, when you're working for yourself you have a shit ton more flexibility, but I will guarantee you that if you do not set a start time, you will basically get nothing done. You have to learn to hold yourself accountable, there's no way around it.

NUMBER THREE is all about perception and forcing people to know who you are. Most people, by nature, are not going to come up to you and say "hello". How many times have you been walking somewhere, passed by another person and made eye contact, yet neither of you say "hello"? Most times, one person will look away quickly and just keep on walking. When you don't know anyone in a new environment, be proactive and force people to know who you are. Walk up to them, say "hello", and them give them your name, and ask theirs.

Now, I'll admit I'm not the best at remembering names so I would write down visual references to remember. The powerful part is when you see them again, say "hello" and USE THEIR NAME! You would be amazed at how much better service and perks you get by just using people's names. When was the last time you were talking to a clerk at a desk or a cashier at the grocery store and used their name when talking to them? Something just as simple as "How is your day going (name)?" When was the last time you remember anyone doing that? I guarantee you it's not very often, and if you are one of the ones that do, you know how powerful it is.

I've seen people get free upgrades to first class on a flight, free upgrades to suites in hotels and big discounts on products that they had no coupon for. It really is that powerful and by remembering and greeting people by their name, you are instantly recognized as someone who gives a damn about someone else. It's powerful for you when someone else has the feeling you have interest enough to know and use their name.

Again, the goal here is perception and forcing people to know who you are. You can bet when they see that you remember their name, they're not going to forget yours!

NUMBER FOUR is a no brainer. No matter if it's your job or if it's a group of people who are on another level than you, you want to make yourself known amongst them. This is just like branding in marketing. You are forcing your peers to remember who you are and by doing so it makes them easier to notice the other things you do.

Many people try to hide from their peers or boss, believing that if they stay clear of them, the less potential of a problem they have. This is total and complete ass-backwards thinking! If they have a decision to make on who goes or stays, or if they want to do a project with someone, who do you think has the better chance? The one they know or the one they don't? The answer is pretty simple, but too many people screw this up and it costs them. Of course, they then wind up complaining that someone else got the position. I can't stand it when people who blame other people for their lack of success. That other person was just willing to find a better angle or work harder.

I guarantee many people reading this are shaking their head at my **NUMBER FIVE**. The cooks and the dish crew? Really? Most people think, "who cares" and *that* is the problem. The blueprint is a list of things to do. In my case, to get a station that I want serving the best tables. So what do the cooks and dish crew have to do with it? It's that kind of thinking that allows people like me to jump right ahead of all of those who think the cooks don't control your entire night! I'll explain why and then explain it in the realm of business so you can see just how powerful it really is.

Going by my list and job at the time I wrote it, the cooks flat out make or break your night. The actual work part of being a server is a joke, and yes, I can say that because I did it for years. The only thing I did was greet the customers at my table station, take a drink order, food order and punch it into the computer system. That is it, other than refilling drinks! The REAL work is done by everyone else, thus you're about to understand why getting in good with the cooks is a good idea.

No matter how good of a service I gave a table, if the food was cooked wrong, late, early or anything in between, it reflected on me. I was the point of contact between the customer and their food. The customer doesn't really care that I didn't cook the food or that the kitchen was backed up. I was the one who was supposed to be taking care of them. This is the angle that most people just don't open their eyes to and see, and yet it's in place at any business out there, no matter if it's your own or not.

As long as I was in good with the cooks, my food was never late and I had the ability to get something fast if I needed it. I forgot to turn in a ticket? No problem, I simply told the guys I fucked up and forgot to turn it in. They would move other people's food out of the way just to get mine out in time. I had something that was cooked wrong? Simple, they simply grabbed something else that was cooking for someone else and gave it to me. They're completely backed up and running late on tickets and I need a desert ASAP? "Not a problem Zim, I got you right now, man." That was the answer that came.

That's right, they would STOP what they were doing and help me out immediately, all because I would do the things that nobody else was doing for them. Saying "hello", calling them by name, asking THEM if I could do anything for them to make their shift go easier. The cooks have the hardest jobs in the restaurant hands down, and they get paid shit wages for the amount of work they do. Here I was making a hundred bucks a night in cash from tips and they were lucky to make sixty bucks before they got whacked in taxes.

The dish crew? Okay, they honestly did nothing for me to

make my shift go easier but use your head for a minute. The dish crew was pretty much the starting point of a job for every single cook on the line. A rite of passage if you will.

Most all kitchen staff starts in that dish pit, so if I could get in good with them before they ever made it to the line, how much easier was it to already have them on my side right from the jump start, right? I watched it night after night, how other servers would treat them like shit because they were the "dish crew" and their jobs had zero effect on their own. That all changed when they graduated to the line though, and you can bet they didn't forget the treatment when they got there.

So I went out of my way to help them stack plates, to run glasses and to get them drinks. I even bought them dinner a time or two. Trust me, it paid off 100 times over when I needed something in return.

Some people reading this are likely thinking to themselves, "what the hell does that have to do with me running my own business or working in the job I have now?" If that's you, do me a favor and punch yourself in the stomach as hard as you can, because you're an idiot!

The point is, that in any situation, no matter if it's a job or your own business, there are "cooks" and "dish crew" that can make or break your success. There is not one business person who "does it all" and is successful on a scale that's worth a shit. Everyone has people they rely on to help make a business profitable. Your job is to FIND those people in your situation and treat them like gold.

In return, they will not only work harder for you, they will help catapult your success ten times over. They'll do it happily because you actually give a shit and in return they give a shit about you. I don't need to explain why a group of people who give a shit about each other is a powerful force. If I do, just put this book down now and go back to watching TV.

NUMBER SIX on my list is very similar to the one above. The bus boys made sure my tables were cleaned off. If there are two tables that are dirty and they're going to clean mine first every single time, who do you think is going to make more money? Again, I asked them if I can get them any drinks, help them with anything or just how they were doing. Do you think anyone else did that? Not many, and not with the regularity that I did. They knew when I walked in, that I was going to come over to them and say "hello". In return, they made damn sure if there were ten tables open and mine was one of them, that mine was getting cleaned first.

I'm not sure if you notice or not, but I've already laid the groundwork to keep what gets most people in trouble, out of it. My food was never late. If there was a problem, it was solved immediately. My table were instantly cleaned, which gave me the biggest turn ratio of the staff and that meant that as long as I could keep drinks refilled, that my customers were always very happy. Partner that with the fact I made it a purpose to say "hello" to everyone, including the bosses, and there was no way I didn't stick out. Now let's continue the ground work and start building the blocks even higher.

In **NUMBER SEVEN**, we look at the hostesses. They are another pawn in the game, and no matter where or what you do, there is always a person in the "hostess" position. This could be a high level executive's secretary. It could be someone else's assistant, or simply someone who sets a schedule for something or someone. The bottom line is, if you get in good with the appointment setter, you're golden!

By being in the good graces of the hostesses, I was able to get better tables. I was able to stop getting tables sat when I was ready to leave, and even so far as being asked which table I would rather have. This was unheard of for the most part because usually the hostesses are doing nothing but getting harassed by the wait staff. I just went a better route. I'd help bus tables if they were slammed on a wait and the bussers were behind, I'd help seat customers and I'd sometimes even try and talk down customers who were giving them a hard time. I helped the hostesses, but they helped me so much more because of it.

Now that I had pretty much everyone else squared away and working for me, I would then turn to the other members of the wait staff and help them.

In **NUMBER EIGHT**. When I had a free minute or two, and I had plenty, I would run food out to tables for the other servers. They loved this because it helped them out if they were busy. It kept their tables happy, which in turn kept them happy with me. So now, if I needed a favor or needed to ask someone to run my food for me, it wasn't a question of if it was going to happen, it was just a question of which one was going to do it.

28

Again, in the business world, no matter if it's at a job or your own business, there are people in these positions. Help them out and they will all help you. You can't look at it as if they "owe" you either because not all will reciprocate with you. You have to look at it as it's just another piece in the puzzle.

NUMBER NINE is the one that brings all the pieces together. If you are doing numbers one through eight, I will guarantee that the managers have already taken notice of you. So in number nine, I made sure that I put myself in direct line with the managers to get the maximum benefit of all the other things I was already doing. This does two things for you and both are extremely important.

First it showed them I was a team player. Now, don't get it mixed up in that I was all about the "team" here and making sure everyone had a smooth shift. You'll only get so far in whatever it is you want to do if your concern is the "team". Think that's a messed up statement if you want, but any true entrepreneur is out for one thing and one thing only - to get what they want (as an individual). This was, no doubt, about ME and making sure I was doing everything in my power to get myself what I wanted. My doing what I was doing was making THEIR night easier, and from that, anyone will take notice.

The second thing it does for you is that it shows them that not only are you doing all of the other things I mentioned in the previous numbers, but that you are also on top of your own shit enough that you make time to help THEM out as well. Taking the managers plates from the kitchen window wasn't that big of a deal really, and it's not something the managers did themselves. They would ask one of the servers or bus boys coming down the line to do it for them. No big deal, but I made it so they didn't have to ask anyone. I just walked by and did it! If you notice the list, I also had an exact number of times I was going to do it as well, just to make sure it got noticed.

Even that is not a huge deal, but here is where it really pays off. All the other servers and bus boys started to see I was just grabbing those plates as I walked by. I didn't have to be asked, and I didn't say anything to the managers when I did it. I just grabbed them. What did everyone else start doing? They started grabbing them as they walked by, too! It got to the point it became almost like a competition as to who was going to get the plates for the managers. The question is why did they do it if I was already doing it? The answer is simple and a leverage point that has been in place since the beginning of time. It was all about their ego.

While I couldn't see the expression on the managers faces when I grabbed the plates, I already knew what it was. You can bet everyone else saw it though and they wanted some of that expression pointed in their direction, too. There was no way they were just going to stand around and let me get all of it when something as simple as grabbing some plates could produce it. It was too late for them though, because I was already the leader and they were now my followers, and the managers knew it!

You're probably thinking to yourself that nobody likes a suck up, and you're absolutely correct, but what you're probably missing is that everything else I was already doing kept me from ever being seen as one. Cold, hard and really damn calculated! I had already set myself up to the point where I was helping everyone, without really even trying. I was just doing things for everyone that really take no more time than a couple seconds, and because of that, nobody ever looked at it as anything more than being a really nice guy. THAT is the power of mapping things out instead of just going off what you "think" you should do.

NUMBERS TEN TO FIFTEEN are nothing more than backing up what I had done in numbers one through eight. As long as I did those things, there was never a reason for anyone to think I was anything more than the consummate team player. Number nine was the one that would wrap up the deal of getting me what I wanted faster than anyone else.

Finally, **NUMBER SIXTEEN** was the final piece of the list and that was to ensure that I left nothing out of place that I could get in trouble for. The last thing you want to do is go through your plan, and then leave yourself open to hurt your efforts by not doing your own job. Regardless of how well you do the other parts, if you don't have your position in tip top shape, it won't matter. You'll always be the person who has to be told to "clean up your mess" like you're supposed to.

My list is literally the formula to get you pretty much whatever you want, no matter where you are. You can apply it to being self-employed or to your work in the corporate world. The goal, no matter what your job or position is, is to get yourself what you want! Never lose sight of that, and never fail to plan it out in detail.

Chapter 4

The Awakening

This chapter may be the one that gives people the most problem because it's not the easiest thing for many to do. Especially these days, when people are more and more comfortable with blaming others for their problems. Hell, they're even teaching our kids this crap. Since when did we start giving out trophies for the team that comes in last place? When did we start telling people that if you have a problem with something that someone is doing, that they should go and tell someone? Why is it such a bad thing for people to get offended, especially in the last ten to fifteen years? When did bullying become so bad that we have kids committing suicide in record numbers? In my opinion, the answers to every single one of those situations is complete bullshit and it's all being spearheaded by a bunch of bullshit propaganda with ulterior motives. Forgive me for a moment as I rant on these things, but you'll see exactly what I'm talking about when I tie it together. Plus it's my book, so I can write whatever I want.

If we give out trophies to the last place team so they'll not feel so bad about losing, what the hell are we doing to make them want to do better? What we're telling you here is "it's okay to lose because you're going to get a trophy just like the first, second and third place teams".

To anyone who has ever had a competitive bone in their body, that's a lot of bullshit! Losing is supposed to make you want to work harder! Losing and getting nothing should make you want to skip that movie to go work on your game, or your skills or whatever it is so when you get another opportunity, you're fucking ready! It's supposed to push and drive you to work on getting better.

If you lose, you don't deserve a damn trophy! You deserve the crappy feeling you get when you lose. For the ones that are motivated by the crappy feeling of losing, to get better and then STAND UP as a winner next time! The ones who get motivated to not ever feel like that again are the future leaders, entrepreneurs and people who will change the world. While the ones who want to complain are the same ones who will suck your hard earned tax money down with that pack of cigarettes they're smoking. Cigarettes that were probably bought with a welfare check.

The other side of that is, what is it doing to the ones that actually won? They got a trophy because they earned it. What does it tell them when they see the last place team being celebrated just like they are? You get first place you deserve to walk around with your head held high and a little strut in your step. You EARNED IT! You worked hard and sacrificed. You earned that trophy and you earned the stares of desire from everyone else watching you hold the trophy in hopes one day that will be them. Part of that gets lost when some of your glory gets taken away because someone doesn't want the others to feel bad.

Yes, yes, I know. I am sure there are some of you reading this and saying to yourself "You're wrong. It's about the growth of them as a person..." and some other garbage. Make no mistake, you didn't win second place, you LOST first place! There is competition in life from the moment we're able to interact with others. It's natural, it's part of who we are as a species, and if you think for one split second that in the business world, anyone is going to feel bad for you because you're not as good as someone else, you're in for a long road as someone's secretary or errand person. No matter how much you hate it, dislike it, disapprove of it, or wish it would go away - it's not going to. Deal with it!

Which brings me to people being offended. You know what happens when someone gets offended? Are you ready for this? Because it's going to shock the shit out of you...

What happens?

NOTHING!

Nothing happens when people get offended, it's a choice whether something offends you or not. You certainly don't all of a sudden come down with cancer because someone offends you. You don't wake up the next morning and have three arms, lose a few fingers, get massive headaches, get a runny nose, develop an allergy to humans or any other stupid thing you can think of due to someone offending you! I hope some things in this book offend a lot of people.

Being offended should bring about a CHANGE in YOU! Too many people want to run and complain to someone else when something happens that they don't like. And before you start throwing this book down, realize I'm not talking about things such as racism, mentally or physically handicapped people and children, and things of that nature. I'm talking about when people complain about the use of curse words in the work setting or complain that one gender gets a better job than the other. I am talking about things of that nature that people love to complain about because it's easier than taking a look in the mirror and recognizing what they're really upset over. Being offended brings about change in a person and it's one of the most powerful things that can happen to you. I look to find something that offends me almost every day and yet I rarely find anything!

And why in the last fifteen years or so, are more and more kids committing suicide and giving the reasoning of bullying? Are we really going to pretend like bullying just started? It has been around for as long as any of us can remember, but the problem is that it used to be dealt with in a totally different way than it is now. We used to teach our kids that if they are being bullied, to stand up for themselves and to smack the bully in the mouth the next time they messed with you. Yes, you may very well get your ass whipped for it, but that bully will leave you alone after that because they know you're not going to just lay down and take it. Not anymore!

For the last fifteen years or so, we've taught people that they should run and tell someone. Guess what happens when you run and tell someone most times?

… wait for it….

… wait for it…

… the answer again, is NOTHING!

Very rarely does anyone do anything at all, other than talk about it. What good does that do? All talking about it does is make a person feel better for a few minutes until it happens again. Then they go tell again and they talk about it some more. It's no wonder you see kids shooting each other and getting so worked up that they commit suicide these days. Nobody does anything other than complain and talk about it so they get to the point they just can't take it anymore, and they snap! Wind up anyone to that kind of pressure level and they'll snap, too.

So at this point you are probably thinking "What the hell is the point of all of this?

It's simple and it's something that everyone should not only be taught, but also something they should take it to heart because what I mentioned above is the truth!

The point is, right now, at this very moment, you need to accept the fact that YOU, and YOU ALONE are responsible for your success or failure, for your happiness or unhappiness. It is on you to dictate your surroundings, your ambition, your drive, your determination, your want, your will, and your attitude. At the end of the day, no matter how good of friends you have, no matter how tight your family is, no matter how smart other people think you are or anything else you can put in with those words, the only one you can 100% honestly and truly rely on, is yourself!

Nobody else is going to give it to you, nobody is going to hand it to you, you are not going to wake up and it's all of a sudden going to be there. Regardless of how much you're told you're loved, how they've got your back or anything else, you must remember that they have their own lives, too! Your friends and your family will not do this for you. Your life is on you.

From this moment forward, you must be willing to admit that you, and you alone, are responsible for your success and you are also responsible for your failures. No more complaining, no more whining, no more blaming things on other people and no more elf-pity. Anything other than you taking full responsibility for your outcome is an excuse, and that from this point on, you won't tolerate excuses – especially your own.

This is a huge step for many people because they have to reprogram their way of thinking.

Where you once could just blame someone or something else, you no longer can. Get rid of that crutch to lean, the one that you have gotten so comfortable with, and be ready to wade into unknown waters. I will welcome you to the deep end because that is where the big fish swim! Successful entrepreneurs, business owners, online marketers and those like them all have this one thing in common. They blame no one for their problems and they wait for no one to come and save them.

Understand that excuses are no longer an option, and you'll have to carry on all by yourself if you have to, regardless of who is trying to hold you back.

The successful ones are those built to not accept what is told to them without finding out for themselves. They are few, yet they are many and they all take full responsibility for the workings and outcome of their lives.

Now it's your turn. From this moment on, let there be no more excuses.

When you've reached this state of mind, it's time to let everyone else know where that line is. This won't be easy either, especially for those who have significant others, children or other relationships, but you have to do what you have to do.

But like it or not, the next part, just as this part, must be done, which takes us to the next chapter...

Chapter 5

Debbie Downer and Negative Nancy

There are not too many things I dislike more than people who don't take responsibility for their own wellbeing and state of mind. However, what drives me even crazier is that there are people out there, who because of their own shitty state of mind, think it is okay to constantly be negative about what everyone else is doing.

"You shouldn't do that."
"You need to get a real job."
"You need to stop chasing that dream."
"That's never going to work"

… and all of the other bullshit these people spout out of their mouths. The funny thing is, these people usually come in two different forms.

The first, shockingly enough, are the ones who have actually done something impressive. They've gone from nothing to something. They grinded it out, they made sacrifices and they are usually fairly well off, money wise.

What I never understand about these people is that they usually took some sort of risk or chance at some point that got them to where they are now. They either quit their job, started their own company, bought into another company or something like that. None of which would be considered the "smart" thing to do by most people.

Yet when it comes to someone else attempting the same

path they once chose, they complain. Why the hell do they open their mouths and tell other people they shouldn't be doing it?

Did they forget that they most likely had people telling them the same things when they were in the same position? Has success also had an effect on their memory?

Most times, this set of people are family members who just don't want to see their sons or daughters go through the same struggles they went through. Even though they came out on the right side of things, they remember the hard times it took them to get there, and they don't want the same struggle for their kids. Fair enough... kind of.

I've got three daughters, and of course I don't want them to live on three hours of sleep for two years trying to build something. It's not healthy, it's not normal and it's certainly not a guarantee of success. I do know, however, that there's no way I could stand in their way if they wanted to take that task on.

First of all, I'd be a hypocrite and secondly, it would be pretty cool to see any of the three of them have that kind of drive. What I would never do is discourage them. This is what baffles me so much with this set of people. How the hell can you give anything but encouragement to someone trying to break free for a better opportunity for their own life?

Especially when you can remember how you felt with the people around you giving you the negativity about your own choices.

But as I said, most times these are family members. I have not seen too many kids, who at some point tell their parents "piss off, I'll do what I want" and they do so regardless of how their parents feel. It's kind of a rite of passage and it is one I actually look forward to from my own kids. It will show me that they are getting independent and thinking for themselves. This is the natural order of things. It is how people grow.

It's the second set of people that really get my blood boiling. It's the ones who are so upset with their own lives, the way things are going for them, that they are so negative all of the time and it brings everyone around them down. They're always complaining about something or telling you how you should do things, yet when you look at their own success, all you see is mediocrity!

These people need to be told to "shut up". They should take their negativity, their "poor me" attitude, the idea that their mediocrity is a license to tell other people who are trying to change things and shove it up their ass. How are they any kind of authority on telling anyone how to, or what to do, on anything other than being mediocre!

Every time I'm around someone like that and I hear them whining about something, it's like someone scratching their nails down a chalk board. I just want it to stop.

This is as ass-backwards as a Catholic priest trying to tell someone how a marriage should work. I mention it here because it is something that actually happened to me. My wife's family are Catholic and they wanted us to be married in a Catholic church. Honestly, I could have cared less, but if that's what they wanted I was willing to go through whatever I had to, so it would be allowed. One of the things was to meet with a priest and listen to him talk about what marriage was all about. What happened was that I quickly figured out this was nothing more than an opportunity to get me to put money in the offering plate and semi-berate me for not being a Catholic. Well, I'm the wrong person to get on like that, especially with religion.

I finally got fed up with it and asked him what he actually about marriage. "You're a priest, who is not allowed to get married correct? And you were taught by another priest who was also not allowed to get married, right? And most likely, that guy was also taught by another priest who was not allowed to be married? So my question is, what the fuck do you really know about marriage other than what you were taught by some guy who wasn't allowed to get married, who was also taught by another guy who was not allowed to get married."

Needless to say, he didn't like that at all and we didn't get married in that church. I was not going to sit there and listen to his negative bullshit, especially on a subject he really knew nothing about! I immediately removed him from the situation, and that is exactly what you need to do in this step!

This won't be easy, but it has to be done.

From this moment on, you must not, you will not, succumb to other people's negativity. You will not allow their decisions or their views on what it is you are doing, sway you from the path that you've chosen. You will not allow their opinions to sway you from the path you have decided that you need to go down. A path that you have now planned out, that you are now working toward, not only physically but mentally.

Anyone who is not willing to support you in your decision, you let them know where that line is, and then let them know that you will not allow them to cross it. You must let them know there will be serious consequences if they do, and that you fully intent to act on them.

This means anyone and everyone!

By this I mean family, spouse, boyfriends, girlfriends, friends, co-workers and anyone else that you may come into contact with. You are already busting your ass, and the last thing you need or deserve, is some jack ass who is content or upset with their own lives trying to tell you how to live yours.

Let me talk about being content for a minute here, too, because not everyone's negativity will be due to lack of their own state. Being content is fine for some people, and there's certainly nothing wrong with it. If someone has reached a point in their life that they are content with their job, home and surroundings, then more power to them. HOWEVER, that does not mean that because they're content that everyone else in their life has to be. If they do, that's just being selfish with their lack of wanting their "contentedness" interrupted.

Just as you are making a change, your change will potentially mess with their contentedness and most will do whatever is within their power to protect it. Don't let this sway your change. You deserve the right to make changes in your life without someone else trying to hold you back because they're trying to hold on to what they want in theirs. We all make sacrifices, but the last thing you want is to be eighty years old and to look back and say "I wish I would have..." That will be a shitty feeling because there won't be time or opportunity to go back and fix it.

If you really want some clarity, spend some time with older people who are in their eighties and older. Ask them what their biggest regrets are, and I'll guarantee you almost all of them will tell you about the things that they didn't do. They'll say they wished they did more things when they had the opportunity to do them. They knew they could do better or do something different. They wanted to do something different, but they didn't because they were either too scared at the time, or they didn't want to upset the balance. As they look back on it now though, they'll almost all tell you, "If I knew then what I know now, I would have done it".

Learn from that! Your parents probably told you many things when you were younger that you just blew off. "Yeah, sure, mom and dad, whatever. I hear you, but what do you know". We've all said it and we've all thought it. But damn it, tell me at some point almost everything they told you was right to an extent! Of course you don't realize that until you're much older than when you heard it, but you recognize the knowledge they had. You were just too young and defiant to see it at the time.

THINK though! These older people have been there, done

that, just as our parents had. Don't make the same mistake twice. Listen to them and then make sure that's not you in that chair at eighty years old filled with regrets.

When you do this step, you must do it with a solemn vow to yourself. Imagine yourself being a knight of the olden days taking a scared oath.

> *"There is no room whatsoever for the allowance*
> *of any negativity in my decision making from now on.*
> *I will remove any and all things that stand in my way.*
> *I have drawn my line and I will let it be known.*
> *There will be dire consequences for any*
> *who dare to attempt to cross it."*

It is a very powerful step and promise to yourself.

Do it.

Chapter 6

Your Own Private Movie

No matter how much people want to downplay the power of your mind. The facts speak for themselves. What you think is reality, will turn into reality if you believe it. Now, let me clarify that for a minute. I don't believe in this bullshit that you can think you're going to be rich and actually believe it and then it just magically happens. That's bullshit and it doesn't work. If that was the case, everyone would be rich from just standing around and thinking "I'm rich" until it happens. It takes work and effort, but that work and effort is what I'm outlining for you in this book.

I do, however, absolutely believe that when you combine the power of the mind and the power of the effort, there's nothing you can't accomplish. Your mind is a powerful thing and if you train it properly, it's the best weapon you have. Not only in business, but in health, and life in general.

We all know someone who thinks the worst is always going to happen in every situation. Then of course, it does happen to them pretty much every time. Why? Because they're expecting it to happen! We also know that one person who just seems to be happy all of the time and expects the best out of every situation. Of course, that person usually does get the best out of whatever situation they're in. There's a problem with those two types of people though.

The first type expects the worst, and while they usually get just that, they walk around scared or upset all the time. They wake up wondering "what the hell is going to happen to me today that is going to suck?" That's no way to live and it will put you in an early grave. Who wants to walk around miserable all day just waiting for something bad to happen? I sure don't.

The second type expects the best and usually gets it. The problem is, when they expect the best and wind up with the worst or less than expected, they get flustered and upset. Not always, but these people have a real hard time dealing with a crisis usually. They're so used to being positive that when something really bad happens, they often can't handle it. They're not used to it and don't know what to do.

Then we have the third type of person, which is the one you want to be like. This person is seen as "lucky" all of the time. This person always gets the promotion or closes the deal. They seem to always been on top of everything they do and everyone wishes they had that persons kind of mojo. I'll tell you right now, this is not luck, no matter how bad you want to believe it. You've heard the phrase "luck favors the prepared mind"? Well it's absolutely true, and people like this make their own luck!

This is where being prepared by doing the steps outlined in this book along with what I call *your own private movie* blend together.

Throughout history, there have been hundreds of examples of what I'm about to tell you, and most of the examples are based on people who were at the top of their profession.

Jim Thorpe, who is widely regarded as the best athlete ever, was sitting in a chair with his eyes closed when someone asked him what he was doing. His response was, "I'm winning the Olympics. Over and over again in my mind I'm winning the Olympics".

Gary Player was the best golfer on the planet at one time. There are stories of him told by his roommates, that they were often awoken buy Gary staring at himself in the mirror and repeating over and over "I'm the greatest golfer on the planet".

Tiger Woods, this generation's best golfer by a wide margin, has said he's never hit a shot he hadn't already played in his mind.

Michael Jordan has said he constantly imagined himself dominating a basketball game and making the final shot to win.

There are hundreds more like this, but the one thing they all have in common is that they all have it happen in their mind prior to it actually happening. Now, this is where shit like *The Secret* will tell you to just imagine it and it can happen. What a load of bullshit! Every single one of those people I just mentioned busted their ass to have the success they had. What they did was blend the mental power of their mind with their actual work and THAT is how it happened.

I'll be upfront about it, and tell you that you're not going to master this right from the start. Just like anything else worth doing, it's a process you go through, and there are steps you're going to take. Some might start off better than others, while some may be able to jump right to the best method without a problem. I don't know which you'll be, but it's important you be honest with yourself and not jump to the next step until you're ready.

When we talk about mind power, I mean the ability to actually visualize something that hasn't happened yet. You visualize something you want to happen. Something you're working towards with your tasks, goals and progress. You're already busting your ass to make it happen, but here's that little bit extra that gives it a push.

The key is to not just visualize it in your mind, but to actually make it so real in your mind that's it's happening right at that very moment.

You eventually want to get to the point that you can smell what the room smells like, hear your breathing, feel your heart beat, and feel the temperature in the room. Everything as if it was actually happening right at that moment. You want to get to the point you are looking through your own eyes at other people in the room. You can look down and see your hands, your clothes; you can feel the way your clothes fit.

We've all had this before in our dreams. We've all had a dream that was so real, when we woke up, it took us a second or two to recognize that it wasn't real. THIS is the level of visualization you want to be able to get to and it's the level of visualization that the top athletes have mastered.

When *Jim Thorpe* said he was winning the Olympics in his mind, he was visualizing it as if it was actually happening right then. He was feeling the adrenalin of the race, the roar of the crowd, the push of his competitors, the feeling of crossing the finish line first and by how far he was ahead of the second place finisher. He continued to visualize all the way up through the medal presentation. He could feel the feeling the gold medal being placed around his neck. The weight of it, the smell of it, and the goose bumps he got from hearing the crowd cheer. It was real, even though it was in his mind.

What he gained from that is that when the actual race happened, he had already won it in his mind so many times, he didn't have to deal with all of the pre-race jitters, the nerves or wondering what would happen. He *knew* he was going to win, his body knew exactly what do it because it had been there so many times before in what felt like the actual event.

Your body can't tell the difference between reality and a dream. When your dreams are that real, and when you can visualize that same way, your body can't tell either. THIS is where the phrase "if you can believe it you can achieve it" comes from, yet nobody ever explains it that way.

The reason this is so powerful is the more you do it, it's like forming a habit. The body doesn't realize it's not real due to how well you visualize. It's as if you were actually doing it. This is what you're going to achieve.

There are three different levels of your "movie" and each is more powerful than the one before it. You must make sure you don't go to a level you can't yet properly achieve however, or you're doing yourself a disservice. It's better to do a level properly than one improperly, even if it's a more powerful form of visualization.

Level One

Level one is as if you are watching a movie of yourself doing something. You close your eyes and picture a big movie screen, just as if you were in a movie theater. On that movie screen, visualize yourself doing exactly what it is you want to achieve. This could be anything that you want to see yourself accomplish. See yourself speaking on stage, going to the bank to cash a million dollar check, getting promoted, standing on a scale and seeing the number you want to have reached, or any other situation you can think of.

Watch and pay close attention to your facial expressions, your body movements and your surroundings on the screen. What you're looking for here is that feeling you get when you're really into a movie that you get emotionally involved. I'm sure you've been so into a movie at one time or another where you forget for a minute it's not real. You feel good when the guy gets the girl or the hero saves the day. You get nervous when the buildup happens and you get on the edge of your seat. You know it's a movie, but you're emotionally invested in it. That's the feeling you want to get yourself into when you're watching a movie of yourself in your mind.

This is your own private movie, so make it play exactly how

you would want it to and make sure to feel yourself becoming emotionally invested in it.

Level one is very powerful so don't underestimate it just because there are two other methods. This level alone can do wonders for making things change and getting what you want. So please, I'll ask you again, start with this one first and see how well you can do it. When you can get to that emotionally invested state like you do when you're into a good movie, keep doing it for at least seven days in a row before moving on to level two.

Level Two

In level two, instead of watching yourself in a movie, you're going to watch yourself as if you were in the stands or in the audience, live. Just as in level one, you are controlling what you're seeing yourself do, so make it exactly what you want. In this level though you want to make it so real it is as if you are actually there, live and in person. Concentrate on how you feel watching yourself do what it is you've chosen to see. Watch yourself breathing, your movements, your and facial expressions. Feel your emotions and take in your surroundings.

Try and feel it as if you were right there watching yourself in person and exactly how that would feel. Feel how proud of yourself you are, how important it makes you feel to see yourself doing exactly what you want, Notice the way the way others are looking at you and how that makes you feel. Notice the smell in the room, your breathing and pay attention to your own emotions as you watch yourself. The goal here is to make it so real that it's as if it's actually happening.

Level two is obviously more powerful than level one because you're actually putting yourself in the situation. It's no longer something you're watching on a movie screen, you're actually IN the movie watching it happen. At this level you can actually feel the atmosphere and sense the smells in the room. It's true emotion. To your body and mind, it's the same as when you were at that professional sports game or in the audience as your favorite band played or something important in your life happened. When you can make this type of visualization happen, keep at it for at least seven days before moving on to level three.

Level Three

Level three is the most powerful level and one that may take you a little time to master. It's worth every second you put into it though, because you can truly make magical things happen here. In level three, you are no longer watching yourself. You ARE yourself. At this level of visualization, everything happens as if you were watching it through you own eyes, just like you're reading this right now. Through your own eyes, as if it was happening right now, be IN the situation you want to be in.

Notice everything you can here. How your feet feel on the ground, how your breathing is, how your clothes feel on your body, how you emotionally feel right at that moment and every other little detail you can recognize. The goal is to make it feel so real that you're body and mind can't tell the difference between the visualization and reality. This is the exact same state of consciousness as those dreams that are so real when you wake up it takes you a second to recognize it was a dream.

The reason this is so powerful is because it's feeding your subconscious mind exactly what it needs to have to make whatever it is your seeing actually happen. Think about learning to drive and what that was like in the beginning. After a while, you don't even think of working the brake and the gas and how it functions. You don't think about turning on your turn signal or stopping at a red light, it just happens. You've driven so many times at this point that many times you can actually go 10 miles and not remember what you saw or how fast they went by. This is because you've done it over and over and it's all controlled by your subconscious mind now. You don't even have to think about it, you just do it.

Level three is doing the exact same process and it's the same process thousands of professionals have used to achieve what they want. You visualize things in a way that is so real, your body believes it is really happening. The more you do it, the more your body recognizes it has done it and it becomes completely subconscious. As far as your body and mind are concerned, you've already had that promotion, made that million dollars, created that amazing product or got exactly what you wanted so it's not a huge deal to now subconsciously direct you towards situations to actually make that happen.

The key is getting to a level where there is no difference between the visualization and reality, as far as your mind is concerned. You've already experienced the rush of emotion, the adrenaline, the fear, the worry, the joy, the excitement and the outcome over, and over again. So as you're doing the work to make things happen, your body already knows how to react or adapt in your favor because it's already been through it countless times.

This is a magical place, it really is. Your mind is the one thing that really has no limits. The only person that can control your mind is YOU! No matter what anyone tells you or how they make you feel, your mind is in your control. You have the power to change anything you want, anything, and never let anyone tell you any different.

These three levels have changed lives and they can change yours. They certainly changed mine in more ways than I can count. I have yet to visualize something that I've taken to level three that has not come to be. Obviously, I put the other steps with it because you have to do the work, but when you combine the work with these three levels, it's better than any illusion a magician can do. An illusion isn't real, what these levels can do to change your life is more than real. It's the closest thing to magic you'll ever see.

The key to this is consistency! Just like anything else, the more you do it the better you get at it. This isn't something you can do with a bunch of distractions going on either. You need to set aside some quiet time so you can focus and concentrate without distractions.

From this point, you should practice your visualization EVERY DAY even if it's just for just ten minutes. I like to do it first thing in the morning before anyone is awake, or right before I go to bed. I find that starting off my day with visualization just puts me in the best situation to get the day started right. I've gotten to the point where I can do everything at level three, so when I'm done I'm already on cloud nine. I've already seen and felt what I want to happen, and now that I'm starting my day, subconsciously I'm already working towards it.

Ideally you'd like to get 30 minutes a day to practice and visualize, the better you get at it, the less time you will have to spend doing it. I've got myself to the point now I can do it in about ten minutes. We can all find 30 minutes where we can get some time to visualize, so make it a priority from this point on. It will change your life.

Again, I know you may be reading this saying you don't have 30 minutes. My response to that is you may need to go back and re-read one of the previous steps and make your commitment. Either that or you're still more into the idea of success than actually doing what you need to really make it happen. If that's you, I understand. But you'll wind up working for people like me instead of getting what you want.

Chapter 7

I'm Watching You

I'm sure you've heard the phrase success leaves clues. There are no ifs, ands, or buts about it - it's absolutely true. In this step, it's time you start to recognize those clues that are being left behind by others who are in your field.

For many, this is where the human ego comes in to play. People are, in general nature, jealous and envious. We don't like it when someone is more successful than us. Stop telling yourself "I'm not like that", because you are. You may not outwardly show it or act upon it in a way anyone can see, but we are all competitive by nature and someone doing and getting more than what we do or get triggers emotions inside of us. Those could be envy, anger, sadness or jealousy, but it triggers something in us all. Let me be crystal clear here... KNOCK THAT SHIT OFF!!

It's fine if it motivates you, but there are few people who get motivated by someone else doing better than them. If that's you, congratulations, you're one of the few. Most people go into the "why not me, why them" mind set, and just take a back seat to someone else's rise up the food chain. Your ego is a fantastic thing, but you must use it to motivate you, not hinder you.

Success leaves clues and that's exactly what you're going to start paying attention to from this point on! If someone is doing better than you, that's a GOOD thing! If there's a bunch of people who are doing better than you in whatever it is you want, that's even BETTER! There's an old saying which says, "When the student is ready, the teacher will appear". Well, buckle up because the moment you get your ego to stop working against you and start having it work for you, you'll see all kinds of teachers. They've been there all along.

Instead of being envious of those doing better than you, WATCH exactly what it is that they're doing. You've got a front row seat to see exactly how and what they're doing if you just know where to look.

Watch how they handle the situations that come up all the time. You see, most people don't look at things this way. They just look at the outcome, but they don't see all of the stuff that goes into making outcome happen. Here's an example that you see all the time in the online marketing world...

Someone looking to make a little extra money goes looking for how to make money online on the internet. They come across a sales page that says something along the lines of "Push Button Software Makes $30,000 in 24 Hours."

Now, that either gets someone really excited or really upset. The excited one believes this can actually happen and is going to immediately solve all their money problems, so they buy in right away. The other immediately thinks it's a scam because if you could push a button and make that kind of money, then why isn't everyone doing it? Neither one is actually thinking about what has to go into that to make it happen. They're just looking at the result and then making a conclusion. Remember what I said at the beginning of this book about you already having come to a conclusion of who I am just by judging this book cover? In this situation, both people are wrong!

The truth is, you can absolutely push a button and make $30,000.00 in twenty-four hours. I've seen it done countless times and I've done it myself more than once. What is not being shown is the time and process that goes into it to make it happen. Want to know exactly how to do it? I can explain it one sentence.

Build a massive email list through an auto responder, create a product or promote one as an affiliate, write an email and push the send button. That's it, and yes, you can absolutely make that kind of money with the instructions in that one sentence. Cool outcome, right? Yeah, but the part you don't hear about is what it takes to build that massive email list!

There are a ton of things that have to be put in place before you can just push that send button and make that kind of money. You need an auto responder, you need a good converting squeeze page, you need traffic, you need an incentive for them to give up their name and email address. You need money to pay for traffic, or a good amount of time to bring it in through free methods. You have to create a product that will sell, or you have to find one that sells well enough so that your list of subscribers will be interested in paying for it.

Depending on how much money you have to spend on traffic, the process could take a year before you get enough subscribers to make that kind of money. So yes, that $30,000.00 sounds like a lot of money to get in twenty-four hours, but what if it took you a year to set it up? Is that a lot of money for the whole year, even though you made it all in twenty-four hours? No, it's not.

Is that really all there is to it though? To your average person who lets their ego get in the way and block the proper way to think, yes.

Now let's look at what you should be looking at in that particular situation. Following the success leaves clues format, let's look at not only how to get the most out of that scenario, but how to capitalize on it.

First, you have to have a way to collect the emails which is where an auto responder comes into play. There are self-hosted ones and there are services that provide the ability. How to know which one is this person using? You're probably going to be asking "Well, how am I going to know that?"

Horrible thinking again, FIND OUT!

Sign up to their list!

If they're selling a product on building an email list, I will guarantee there is an opt-in form on that sales page or when you try to leave it. Sign up for their list and when you get an email from them, look at the bottom. It will tell you which company they are using. Research it, look for reviews (although it's hard to find an honest one due to everyone being an affiliate) and see if you're comfortable with it working for you. Don't over think it. Either do it, or don't. Never spend days making a simple decision.

Once you have the auto responder, the next step is to pay attention to what it is they're getting people to sign up for. Are they giving away a free report? Are they giving you the first two chapters of their course? Are they giving you a discount or software? They're incentivizing people in some way to get them to give them their name and email, and you will too. Figure out what that is and then think about why they chose this over something else.

Many times you can go to a tool like *Way Back Machine* (Google it) where you can look at different versions of what that page used to look like. This is very important information because you can see how the person's page has changed over time. Anyone who's good at what they do will be testing things to increase their conversions. Page layout, button color, opt-in incentive, headlines, text, product and more. By looking at past versions, you can already see what they've tested, what they changed and what they're using now. If something is working well, they aren't changing much!

Now you can see what they've used and how it's changed so you know how to start with your own. You've just saved yourself a lot of time testing and spending money. Success leaves clues and you just have to find them. This is the point most would be all excited and just start running traffic. Wrong again, that's not thinking right!

Just because you have a good squeeze page, doesn't mean you just start running traffic. You signed up to their list, so watch (and study) how they interact with you. What kind of emails do they send? How many are they sending a week? How many do they send in the first seven days? Are the emails informative? Are they pushy? Do they just send you something to buy?

This is all critical information because you're going to have some people sign up long before the last ones do. How are you going to keep them engaged? The answer is to watch how the person you're watching does it, and then adapt your own strategy!

Right now, many people who are reading this are pumped up, ready to put up a squeeze page, adjust their engagement and start running traffic, right? Wrong again. You're still not thinking! While you're watching, this is the time you're adjusting your list you created in an earlier step! You're watching what someone else is doing that has got them to where you want to be. You compare what you're noticing to the things you set out for yourself and seeing where you can make changes and improvements.

Then you take that research even further and you look at how they are getting their traffic.

Are they running advertisements? Do they have affiliates? Are they doing ad swaps, webinars, thank you page links and a ton of other traffic strategies? I won't go into all of those, but finding out this information helps you to see how they're doing it and what your options are to do it yourself. Are they friends with these affiliates? Do they cross promote each other or are they well networked in. Do you want to know? Then sign up for the lists of the affiliates and see what they're promoting!

Then you have to start looking at prices, sales pages,

affiliate prizes, contests, affiliate percentages and more. All things that can and should be looked at to give yourself the best opportunity at success.

I could go much deeper into this but I think you get the point here. There are so many clues as to what a person has done to get where you want to be, you just have to pay attention to the things that others don't.

From now on, always watch and analyze the top people that are in your profession or in the area that you are going into and don't just watch them to be nosy. Be calculated! Really pay attention to what it is that gives them that position and success.

Watch their eye movements, watch their hand movements, and watch the tone of their voice. Watch the way they speak, watch the way they talk to and interact to other people. When they talk, is there emotion way up? Is there a lot of passion? Is it very subtle? Are there a lot of hand movements, why are they doing them? What's the reaction that they are getting from people when they are doing these things? And really pay attention and try to figure out what it is, and why they are doing exactly what they are doing.

Something you'll hardly hear anyone tell you is to watch what they do that didn't work out and try to figure out why. What did they do differently or why didn't it work out? How did they react to that? Did they get upset about it? Did they walk away and get depressed or did they go back and figure something else out and come back and try again quickly? What was their response to it? How did they react to it? How did they deal with it?

You pick up so much by really watching and looking for the details in situations. Most people don't do this. They are too busy focusing on what their ego is telling to feel to even notice the lessons happening right in front of them. Don't be that person. It'll hold you back from what you really want!

The popular phrase *"Luck favors the prepared mind"* never rings more true than here. In reality, it's not luck. Luck doesn't have a damn thing to do with it. Luck is an excuse used by people who won't put in the work to make it happen.

Chapter 8

Covert Infiltration

Covert infiltration goes right along with the previous chapter and is an even deeper form of "watching" for the clues which success leaves. It's a proven fact that you will rise or fall to the level of those who you surround yourself with.

If you want to get better at anything, you have to have two things. The desire to work hard to achieve it and to surround yourself with people who are better than you at it. If you talk to any professional athlete, they will tell you the best way to get better is to play against people who are better than you. Yes, they're going to kick your ass for a good while, but you will automatically begin to get better because you're forced to! It's just another way your subconscious mind helps you out. The more you do it, the better you get, and the harder you work.

The other side is, if you surround yourself with players who are not at your level, your game will drop. Sure, you may be the best in the group, but it's not helping you sharpen your game. There's no competition there and you're not going to be anywhere near as focused or driven to grow. You've capped out, so to speak.

In business, it's no different. If all you do is hang around people who make the same amount as you, the chances of you making big jumps in money is slim and none. I'm definitely not saying you should stop being friends with them anymore, which would be a stupid move. I am still better friends with people who make one tenth of what I make than ones that make the same or more as me. However, when it comes to talking about business situations, goals, ideas and any other situation, I'm talking to people who make more. Why? Because they've been there already, and I'm "watching" them as I talked about in the previous chapter!

Now that you've started to watch the ones who are more successful than you, it's time to integrate yourself into their world so you can get a better seat! No doubt some of you are saying that's pretty cold and calculated. Trying to get in with people just because you want to better yourself isn't a reason to be covert about it. To those of you thinking that, have fun punching a clock the rest of your life!

You're damn right it's calculated and you're damn right it's to better yourself. Don't think for a split second the ones you're trying to integrate with didn't do the same thing at some point. It's not personal, it's not underhanded and it's not devious. It's the NATURAL thing that happens with people who are successful. They are drawn to successful people because they KNOW that's where you get the information to rise up to the next level. If you have a problem with that, get over yourself or just accept the fact that you're going to always work for someone else.

Now that I've gotten that out of the way, let me explain something else that those of you who think that is calculated may not have thought about. Yeah, there's that "see you're thinking the wrong way again" thing I keep bringing up.

Business is what we do, it's not who we are! Your business, goals, ideas and dreams are all a means to an end. Nobody says "I want to be in business for the rest of my life!" Nobody says "I want to run a successful business and work eighty hours a week so I can have all the money I want." It's not the business, and it's not the money. It's the happiness, fulfillment or joy it brings you from accomplishing it. At the end of the day, no matter how much money you have, how many friends you have or how successful you are, we're all going to wind up at the same place one day. We all live and we're all going to die. It's the great equalizer!

Knowing this, you have to recognize that just because someone is better than you at your job, got a promotion, owns a company, makes millions or whatever you can come up with, doesn't mean they are not subject to the same joys and sadness you are. This is where connections are made and there's no doubt you won't make them with everyone.

I don't care who it is, if someone wants to talk about the *Miami Dolphins*, I'm in the conversation. This could be a multimillionaire or a homeless person on the street. I'll have that conversation with just as much enthusiasm in either situation. I love football and I have an instant connection to anyone else that loves it.

I'm the same way about golf. I love the sport and I can talk swing theory, short game, *PGA Tour* or anything else anyone wants to talk about golf. I can be in a business meeting, a party, a bar, a BBQ or anywhere else, and when a conversation starts up about it, our "positions" in business or life don't matter.

Here's a little hint... We're ALL like that, and in that, lies the secret!

Due to the "hierarchy" of the business world, the upper levels don't usually hang out with those below them. It's stupid and it reminds me of high school, but that's how it is. So it's your job to find things the people you want to surround yourself with are in to. Again, this goes back to paying attention to things other than the obvious.

Look at a person's watch and see if there's anything special about it. Does it have a sports team on it? Is there a *Mickey Mouse* on it? Many times, gifts are given from grandparents, children, etc. Is it expensive and they're constantly making sure it's in eye sight of others? All of these things provide clues.

Look at their clothes and see if you can notice anything that will give you those clues to who they are. People who play golf usually wear certain brands, as do people who play tennis. Look at their shoes to see if they are wearing runners or dress shoes. Hang around close to their conversations to see if you can pick up anything that you can casually mention in passing, or just as a conversation starter.

You're looking for the "human" element that gives you the opportunity to integrate. Some of you may think you will not find anything that gives you that opportunity, but it's there. You just have to keep looking, it's the key to it all.

I can tell you from personal experience that when you reach a certain level, if it's not one of your friends, then it really depends on what kind of mood you're in on whether or not you're open to talking about business. Honestly, most times when someone starts off a conversation about business, my interest level goes down. I may not know the person very well, or I may not know them at all, but when that's how the interaction starts, my interest in talking to that person goes down. I'm not trying to be mean, either. It's just natural, and it's the same way most people feel. It's honest and if you don't like it, I don't give a shit. You'll have to learn to deal with it because it won't change.

However, if someone starts up a conversation about who the *Dolphins* drafted last year or how many putts they have on average in a round of golf, I'm IN! I'll sit there and talk to them for as long as time will allow. A conversation like that is harmless, and it's always nice to talk to someone who has common interests. There's no barrier, so to speak, as in "this person wants something from me", even if they really do. Let's be honest, we all want something, even if it's just to make a new friend.

Once I speak to a person for a bit, now if they bring up a business question, I don't really mind. They didn't come at me with one right off *Jump Street*. They took the time to actually engage me in something that I was interested in. Due to the fact we have a common interest, I'm already much more acceptable to answering other questions from this person, than someone who just goes right into business stuff.

Hell, I met some of my best friends that way, and it's no different than with anyone else. Look at the friends you have now and tell me that you aren't friends with them because you had common interests when you first met. They wouldn't be your friend if you didn't!

Now let me take it even deeper. Are there any of your friends that you wouldn't be happy to help out with answering a few questions, or maybe putting in a good word? Exactly. And now you see the true point. Yes, it's calculated, but it's also sincere.

You're not going to be friends with someone you don't really like. Just because they make more money than you, or have a better position that you want to get to, doesn't mean those common interests can't exist! Find the ones that you have common interests with, strike up those conversations and make new friends.

Of course these aren't just any new friends. These are the people in the upper level of whatever situation you're trying to climb. Just remember to leave the business stuff out at first and build a relationship based on a common interest.

Here's the key to it all. NEVER go into a situation thinking "what can I do for myself?"

You go into it with the exact opposite! "What can I do to help someone else?"

That's the question you ask yourself! In this situation you're helping someone else connect with you on a common ground. There's no questioning on their part as to what you want or what your long term goal is from the situation. It's just a simple conversation around a common interest. What it does long term for you, is get you remembered when that promotion comes up. It gets you more inside information and it gets you a closer seat to the inner workings of the atmosphere you're in.

Powerful beyond measure.

If you don't think you can do it, there's one other thing you can do.

Once you've surrounded yourself with the people who will force you to step up your game, you do more of what you did in Chapter Seven, and then rinse and repeat.

Chapter 9

It's All About The Climb

No matter how well you do the first steps I've given, you're still going to run into some roadblocks. Nobody just sails smoothly into the lane of success without hitting a speed bump or busting a tire, or two. It doesn't matter how well you prepare, how ready you are or how confident you have become, at some point you're going to struggle. Shit happens, to everyone!

What separates those who make it from those who wind up living the life of a time-clock puncher is the ability to push through. You've got to want it more than just the idea of it. If you don't, this is where you're going to fail!

Almost everyone who reads this book has been on a diet at some point, and almost everyone has quit. Usually people go real good for a week, maybe a month and then out of nowhere... BAM!!! Life happens and throws you right off your schedule. This is where most people quit and say "screw it". They put so much effort into those first three weeks, that when they mess up a day, they can't get back on track.

Look, shit IS going to happen, it always does.

Do NOT let one day ruin all the work you have put in previously. You just pick back up where you left off and you continue. If you want it bad enough, you will get right back on schedule and forget it ever happened.

Now, let's talk about "want" for a minute, as this not something you can learn or create. We touched on it briefly in the chapter about being responsible for your own life, but we're about to get real deep into it now. Whatever it is that you have chosen to do at this point, or if you're simply reading through this book first before doing the steps, let me be crystal clear. You cannot just like the idea of success, you have to truly want it, live it, breathe it and bust your ass for it.

There's great story that a gentleman by the name of *Eric Thomas* told about "want". It was actually in a video that I used to watch almost every morning. I've always had a strong drive, but that video just put me in "go mode" even more. The analogy he used though was a great comparison to how much a person wants something. As you read the story below, ask yourself if your want is as great. If it's not, maybe you just like the idea more than actual end goal you've set.

The story goes like this:

A young man really wanted to be rich. He wanted everything that came along with having more money than he could spend. He wanted the cars, the houses, the lifestyle and the glamor of being wealthy. He wanted it all and began to seek out someone to teach him how to make his want a reality. He comes across this very wealthy man and asks the man if he would teach him how to get rich. The man responds and says "of course, meet me at the beach tomorrow morning at 6:00 a.m. and I'll teach you everything you need to know to be as wealthy as me".

Obviously ecstatic that someone of the man's wealth would so openly share his secrets, the young man went to bed early and dreamed of all the things his soon to come knowledge would provide for him.

The following morning, the two men met at the beach and began to walk. They talked about sports, life, the ocean and many other things. For a couple of hours they just walked up and down the beach talking, but at no time did the man bring up anything to do with how he made his fortune.

Finally growing impatient, the young man ask the guru, "I thought you were going to show me everything I needed to make me rich like you."

The guru looked at the young man and told him to walk with him into the water. The young man had no idea why the guru told him to walk into the water with him, but he did as he was told. When they both got about waist deep in the ocean, the guru told him to put his face down into the water and tell him what he saw. Again the young man couldn't figure out what putting his face down into the water was going to do, but he did as he was told.

As soon as he stuck his face in the water, the guru grabbed him by his neck and forced his entire head under the water as if he were trying to drown him.

Obviously freaked out and scared, the young man began doing everything he could to get his head above water so he could breathe, but the guru was too strong and held him there. Just as his air was about to run out, the guru pulled the young man's head out of the water. Gasping for air and clearly pissed off, the young man screamed at the guru. "What the hell are you doing? You almost killed me!"

The guru's expression changed and the young man could see how serious the man had become. There was a small moment of silence and then the guru asked the young man a question. He asked "When you were under the water just now, and when you knew you were about to run out of air, what was the one thing you wanted to do more than anything else in the world?"

Still annoyed at the guru the young man screamed back at him "Breathe, damn it, you almost drowned me. All I wanted to do was breathe!"

The guru looked back at the young man and told him "You now know exactly what it takes to be successful at whatever level you want to get to".

The young man still puzzled asked him angrily "What are you talking about?"

The guru said to him "When you want to be successful as bad as you just wanted to breathe as I held your head underwater - THAT is the moment it will happen."

That's an extreme way to drive home a point, but it's 100% true. If you don't want it that bad, if you don't want *anything* that bad, then you'll never reach what it is you really want.

You see most people aren't willing to do what it takes. They don't want it as much as they'd want to breathe if they were drowning. But that is what you have to have inside you.

You have to be willing to sacrifice whatever it is to get to where you want to go. If you want something bad enough, you'll do it. If you don't, you simply like the idea of it. You either have this or you don't. This isn't something you can learn, it's not something you can buy and it's certainly not anything anyone can give you. Whatever it is you've chosen, you've got to want it so bad that you would move heaven and earth to make it happen.

When I was waiting tables, I wanted the station I wanted. I did everything to make sure it happened, no matter what it was. If I had to stay late, I did. If I had to take extra tables, I did. If I had to clean up someone else's tables, or work in the dish pit, or do someone else's side work or even come in early, I did it.

When I was doing construction, I wanted off the road and into a management position so I did everything to make sure it happened. I gave up my weekends of relaxation to work. I gave up weekends to clean out the warehouse. I gave up evening hours to clean trucks. I learned how to do payroll. I learned how to do everyone in the office's job. I learned how to order supplies and I learned how to work the computers. I did ANYTHING I could think of to put myself in the position so when it came time to move someone up, there was NO WAY it wasn't going to be me.

When I first started doing internet marketing, I did whatever it took to make it happen. In this case, I gave up pretty much everything! For almost two years, I lived on only three hours of sleep a night. I was still doing construction, working twelve to fourteen hours a day and many times it was six days a week. I would be gone at 5:30 a.m. and lucky if I was home by 8:00 p.m. in the summer time. I would come home, and would be lucky to see my daughter for a few minutes if she wasn't in bed already. I ate dinner around 9:00 p.m., took a shower and then hung out with my wife for maybe an hour before she went to bed. From 11:00 p.m. to 2:00 or 3:00 a.m., I worked on my online marketing.

I was reading everything, looking for who the right people were to follow, trying to get in with them, watching what others were doing and then implementing them myself. I wrote out my list, my tasks and my schedule and I followed it. For almost twenty years, I never missed a *Dolphins* game on TV, but for two seasons, I missed a bunch of them. I was grinding my ass off because I wanted something and I wanted it bad. Nothing was going to stop me.

Two years later, my twin daughters were born. If you have children, you know what it's like with a newborn. Multiply that by two now, and throw in twelve to fourteen hour days with almost no sleep. Yeah, hell on earth is what it was, but I never stopped. I gave up everything I had! I didn't go out anymore, I wasn't watching any football games, I wasn't hanging out with friends and honestly, I didn't miss any of it. Nothing was going to stop me. I wanted it as bad, if not more, than that young man wanted to breathe.

It has to be that way. You will have to make sacrifices. In the end, it's worth it. Let yourself never be that person that sits in their wheel chair at eighty years old and says "I wish I would have given more effort to that when I had the opportunity".

You have that opportunity right now, so take it and ride that shit 'til the wheels fall off!

Chapter 10

The 11th Commandment

This is the shortest chapter in the book because there is no real way to say it other than in plain English. It's also my favorite chapter because it's something I've always prided myself on knowing no one will ever do it better than I do. Bold statement? Absolutely, but I believe it and that's all that matters (more on that later).

You have to work.

You have to work hard.

You have to work harder.

And when you think you've worked hard enough then you need to work even harder!

Why?

Because that's exactly what that person did that's in the position you want to be in.

Nothing is handed to anybody and when you think you've worked enough then you need to spend a little bit longer and work some more.

You have to ask yourself the question, "If I get those things that I wrote down that I wanted, when I reach that point and I have those things, will I look back and say all that hard work that I put in was worth it? The times I wanted to quit, when I wanted to stop, when I wanted to go to bed, when I wanted to watch TV, when I wanted to go to a concert, but I skipped all that stuff. Is where I am now, was it worth sacrificing all those things I gave up to obtain it?"

The answer will be "HELL YES!"

If I gave you a sheet of paper, a blueprint, that listed everything you had to do in the next three years, everything you needed to do on a daily basis and made the promise that at the end of that three years, if you had done them all, you'd get five million dollars, would you take it?

Of course you would, almost everyone would. That's what you're creating here from the material in this book. You're making your own blueprint! You just plug in what you want the end result to be and put forth the effort to make it happen.

The 11th Commandment in my life, and now in yours too, is

Thou Shalt Get To Work!

Chapter 11

The Interrogation

This is one of the most powerful pieces of this method in my opinion because it's not something you can fake. Over the top of my computer where I work, I have a piece of paper with the words "Did you do everything you could today to reach your goal?" To this day, it's the first thing I see in the morning, and the last thing I see before I leave. Every time I sit down to start and every time I am finished with work, I look up at that piece of paper and I ask myself that question. If I've done my work that I mapped out for the day, the answer is easy and I get a feeling of accomplishment knowing I can answer that question no problem. Here's the best part...

You CANNOT lie to yourself! You can lie to your parents, your friends, colleagues and business partners, but there's no way you can lie to yourself. You know when you're full of shit and if you can lie to yourself and truly believe it, you've got a serious problem!

By asking yourself this question, you are forced to answer to yourself. If you don't have the answer, then you know you're not doing what it is you're supposed to in order to reach your goal. You are holding yourself accountable.

While you may think it stops with just answering a simple question, trust me it does not. By asking yourself a question like this and having the answers, you are once again training your subconscious mind. When you hold yourself accountable like this and you have the answer, you are giving yourself positive reinforcement on a daily basis. You feel good when you know you're accomplishing steps and by answering this question, it conditions your mind to continue to believe you're on the right track.

The more you do it, and the more you can consistently answer that question with positive results, the more driven you become without even trying. It should feel good when you accomplish things, so give yourself that feeling every day by asking a question such as the one I do.

On the counter side, it also lets you know when you're screwing up! When you can't answer it, you should feel bad! You're not doing what you promised yourself you would do. You hear so often people talk about how they don't want to let the people around them down. Fuck that! Don't let YOURSELF down and you won't ever have to worry about letting anyone else down.

Right now, take out a piece of paper and write down a question that you will ask yourself every day. Look at it every morning when you start and every evening when you're done working and answer it, honestly. It will become a pattern and you will begin to recognize when you're screwing up even before you're done for the day because you know that question is coming.

It's powerful, trust me.

Chapter 12

The Golden Rule

If you haven't noticed yet, I'm a big believer in the power of combining the power of the mind and real effort. It's been proven over and over again, that when you have those two things in place, there's not much you can't make happen.

Some of you may not do this step and that's okay, but I highly suggest you do it. Many people think it's stupid, weird or pointless, but that's fine. I'll keep those people on my payroll doing tasks I don't feel like doing and the rest of us who do it will continue to drive whatever market we're in.

Just as I mentioned *Gary Player* looking at himself in the mirror every morning and repeating to himself "I am the greatest golfer in the world", I highly suggest you write yourself a pledge that you repeat to yourself. Yes, I know it may seem strange at first to stare at yourself in the mirror and recite some words, but you can't think of it like that.

Here again, you are training your subconscious mind to do exactly what you are telling it to do. The beauty of this is that your subconscious is running behind-the-scenes without you having to control it. In plain English, your subconscious just makes shit happen!

If you are constantly telling yourself you're bad at something, you will at some point actually believe it. Counter that with telling yourself you're really good at something and at some point you will actually believe it. In either example, whatever you tell your subconscious is going to happen.

The key to a pledge, or a mantra if you will, is to keep it present tense! You don't want to say "I am becoming..." or "I will be..." Your pledge always begins with "I AM..."

A few chapters back, I told you nobody will ever out work me. The reason I said that was because for the longest time, that was the first line in my pledge. The pledge I used to say to myself was this...

"Nobody will ever out work me. I work harder and get more done than anyone else. Because I work harder than everyone else, I get exactly what I want and I deserve it."

I said that to myself every morning and every night for three years straight. I never missed a day of doing it. Do I actually work harder than everyone else? Who knows? But I don't really care! As far as I'm concerned, you can put me up against anyone you can find and I will out work them. My mind believes it, I believe it, and I'd put money on it!

Did I start out feeling that way? No, not at all. But I knew that if I worked harder and implemented all the things I'm laying out in this book for you, there was no way all the things I wanted were not going to come to me.

Sure, my wife looked at me like I was crazy a few times, but she certainly didn't complain when what I was doing paid off. Some of the most successful and wealthiest people in the world have been called crazy.

This doesn't have to be a long paragraph either. Just a one or two sentence pledge that you say to yourself every morning and every evening. The key is to really mean it when you say it. Again, your mind doesn't know the difference between reality and visualization if it's strong enough, and while this isn't visualization, it's still reinforcing all of the visualization you're doing.

I highly suggest you do this in front of a mirror and you say it out loud. Don't just glance at yourself while you're saying it either. Look yourself dead in the eyes and say your pledge like it's already happened, as if it occurs every day of your life already. Look at yourself as if you were looking at someone else telling you something extremely important. It's so much more powerful this way than just saying the words.

The more you do it, the more you believe it. The more you believe it, the more it becomes a subconscious thing that just happens. You can tell yourself anything, and if you say it enough, you mean it when you say it and you are doing the work behind it to achieve it, anything is possible.

The final part of this step is more important than any other. It's important not only to this step, but maybe even greater in life, in general. It's only three words, but they are more powerful than any other words I know.

BELIEVE IN YOURSELF.

If you don't believe in yourself, how the hell can you expect anyone else to? The only person who has control over whether or not you can accomplish something is you. If you really believe you can do something, then you can. If you really believe you can't do something, then you won't. All the visualization, pledges and work you're putting in just reinforce your initial belief that you can accomplish something. If you do them all, yet you don't believe in yourself, you're only going to get so far. Yes, you'll get further than most, but you will never reach your full potential.

Maybe right now you don't have that of a strong belief, but by writing out your plans, doing your visualization, saying your pledge, and answering your questions, you soon will. That is exactly what it's designed to do! The more you set goals and reach them, the more you obtain things that you once thought were unreachable, and the more you grow, the stronger your belief will be. When you actually notice you believe you can accomplish anything, it's already been in place subconsciously working for you. That's the beauty of it, and that's exactly how it happens.

And just to quiet that one person that is thinking of something that's physically impossible, no! No matter how much you tell yourself and believe you can grow wings and fly like a bird, it's not going to happen. Put the book down now if that's you, you're not the kind of person this book is for. Don't be late to work on Monday though, or you're fired! :)

Chapter 13

This Is Uncomfortable

Without doing anything else, this step can open up so many doors and opportunities for you it's unbelievable. Most people won't do things that are outside their comfort zone. Everyone has one, but if you try to get someone to do something outside of theirs, it becomes extremely uncomfortable for them. Depending on the person, they either will attempt it, or they'll avoid it.

How much money we make and what our professional job status is can many times be directly related to how comfortable we are. While many people would love to make more money, they don't "feel" like they "deserve" it or are comfortable with what would happen with it. Many are content making fifty-thousand dollars a year and living their life. By content I mean they know exactly what they have coming in, exactly what they can spend, and what kind of lifestyle they can lead on that fifty-thousand dollar a year income.

This is why you see so many people win the lottery and then go broke a few years later. They're not comfortable with that kind of money and they have no idea what to do with it or how to budget it. They've never had that much before and so to them it's a fake sense of feeling that it won't run out. They soon realize that it can run out and before long, they're right back to where they started.

You see examples of what I call "comfort zone prison" every day in life and it starts when we're kids. Think back to grade school when you thought one of your class mates was cute or pretty. You wanted to ask them out but it made you so uncomfortable with what the answer may be that you didn't do it. Hell, that example still holds true to many people in their adult lives! I've seen people go on and on about how beautiful a woman is but they do nothing to let that woman know that they are interested. Rejection is uncomfortable and some people take it harder than others. Here's the golden question though:

WHAT is the WORST thing that can happen?

The worst thing that can happen to you is you are told "no". That's it! A two letter word that simply means it's not going to work in your favor on this one. SO WHAT! Does that mean you're going to stop breathing or instantly die of a heart attack? Hell no, it doesn't. It simply means it's not going to happen right now. Is that really so bad?

I tell people all of the time, "if you want something and the way you're going about it isn't working, then cut the shit and just flat out ask for it". That's right, come right out and ask for exactly what you want. Sure, it's most likely out of your comfort zone, but how comfortable is it to sit there and constantly wonder if it may happen or not? You can spend hours, days, weeks, months and even years wanting something or wondering about something and never find out. So screw the waiting around for it and just come out and ask for it.

The worst thing that's going to happen is you're told "no". Big deal, get over it! If you ask and you're told "no", are you in any different position than you were before you asked?

Nope, you are in the same place. Except that now you know the answer to what you've been talking, wishing, wanting or wondering about and you can finally stop thinking about it. Hell, you could even say you've now got peace of mind from it.

Now take that same situation and instead of being told "no" imagine that you are told "yes"! Has your situation changed now? Absolutely it has, and you're ecstatic about it! Nothing feels better than wanting something, stepping outside of your comfort zone to get it and then succeeding. It's the closest thing to flying you can get feeling wise. Screw cloud nine, you're way above that. It happens more than you think it will, you just have to ask for it.

People are also aware of other people's comfort zones and when you do something that they're not expecting, you've got an advantage. I'll give you an example in the dating world just because it's something many people fear, and it's probably happened to us all.

When I was younger, me and a couple of friends would go out and purposely look for a table of women that had no men sitting at it. Now, most people when they see that would think they're having a girl's night. That they left the boyfriends at home and really don't want to be bothered. Sometimes that indeed was the case, but there was only one way to find out.

Where most men would maybe buy one of them a drink and have someone send it over, we went to the bar, got everyone of them a drink and headed over toward the table. Now, keep in mind we had yet to make any contact with them whatsoever, we just got drinks and started walking over. When we got there, we'd grab a couple of chairs and pull right up to the table they were sitting at. Talk about some crazy looks, we got plenty.

The first thing we'd do is set the drinks on the table, introduce ourselves and say "hello". Obviously, whatever their conversation was before we got there stopped and they would look at us like we were crazy to have just infiltrated their table like that. It completely threw them out of their comfort zone because while they may have been approached multiple times that night, there was a 99% chance it didn't happen in the way we just did it. We didn't ask, we just sat down!

Knowing they were a little shocked at what had just happened, we knew we had to immediately crank up the conversation because we knew it was going to be very awkward and creepy if that moment of silence happened.

So immediately it was "How are you all doing?"

The response was usually something like, "Ummmm, fine".

From there it went one of two ways, it went really well or we basically got told to go away. What most people would think is we got more of the "get gone" response, but the truth is we got to stay and have a good time ten times more than not.

Now, would most people even attempt that or even think it would work out in our favor? Honestly, if I wasn't one of the parties involved, I would say "no", too. The point is, we would have never known if we hadn't tried!

Was that out of our comfort zone? Absolutely, but only the first couple of times that we did it. After that, it was no different than getting in the car and driving to the office.

The only way to deal with a comfort zone in business and in life is to smash the walls down! The best thing you can do for yourself is to do something outside of your comfort zone each day.

Every day, look for something that's outside your comfort zone and then DO IT!

If you do this every day, imagine what it will take to actually make you uncomfortable! Over the course of time, there's not going to be much that you're not comfortable doing.

Think of how effortlessly you do things that you are comfortable with. Now think how much more you can do and achieve if you expanded your comfort zone to double what it is now. Then imagine doubling it again.

Make a point to find something every day and do it. Ask questions when they make you uncomfortable. Flat out ask for things you want from people, and say what's on your mind instead of the thing that will make everyone else comfortable.

Do something you never thought you'd attempt.

Then come back to this chapter in a month and thank

yourself for following it. I guarantee your whole world will have changed and the way you perceive things will have changed with it.

Chapter 14

It's All A Means To An End

All of the previous steps up until now have taught you how to make the most out of any situation you put yourself in. No matter if you want to be a professional athlete or the first billionaire in your family, what you've just read - if you follow it - will give you the best chance to achieve it. The last step in the formula isn't a method, formula or a blueprint. It's not going to make you any better at visualization, it's not going to boost your confidence and it's not going to teach you how to obliterate your comfort zone. What I hope it does is give you is some perspective, but that will be up to you.

Above all else, no matter how much of this formula you follow or how much success you have, always remember to enjoy your life along the way.

Life is so short, and the older you get the more you realize it. The whole reason you will do all of these steps is to have a better life, but enjoy yourself during the process. Don't be old and sitting in a chair and wishing you could have done more or you should have done more or you should have spent more time doing this, that and the other because it would have been a little bit easier or what not. We are all born the same way and we all wind up in the same place. It's the parts in between that you and everyone around you will remember.

Don't get so caught up in work and trying to be successful, that you miss everything else going around you. There will come a time when you will regret that more than anything else. I know because I've already done it. True, I'm only thirty-seven at the time of writing this, but there was a time I was so consumed with making money that I literally blocked out everyone around me.

It's actually fairly easy to do, especially when you start to get your first true taste of success. The moment when it all comes together is one of the greatest feelings in the world. You know you've got it figured out and the more of what you've been doing you can do, the larger the success. If you thought you were working hard before, you will crank it into a whole other level. The problem is you can become so focused on work and making money that you will block out everything else around you.

Success is a great feeling. It's great to know you're providing for your family, that they want for nothing and that you can give them all the things you want. You know what else is a great feeling? Having your kids look up at you with a huge smile when they've asked if you'll read them a story. The times when they want to sit on your lap and watch TV with you. The look on your wife's face when you can plan to take a vacation whenever you want, or when you bring home that overly expensive piece of jewelry you know she wanted.

Just as you know how fast time flies, the times when your kids are young will fly by fast, too. Before you know it, they won't want you to read them a story anymore. You'll be lucky if they even want to talk to you when they're teenagers! Pay attention to these moments, recognize and enjoy them when you can.

Even if you don't have children or a spouse, take the time to enjoy the fruits of your labor. Most of us won't live to be a hundred years old, so you have to figure by the time you turn forty-five, more than half of your life is already over. No matter how old you are right now, don't let any more of it go by without keeping in mind to enjoy it.

They always say that hind sights 20/20. I don't think anyone can argue with that, but as you get older, you see things a lot different than you used to. Think back to when you were a kid and your parents had a house full of people over for Thanksgiving. There was family, friends and their children. Of course, there was the 'adults table' and the 'kids table'. I remember thinking to myself "This is how it is, how it's going to be when I'm older, I guess. I'll have my own kids, we'll have holidays like this. I will have a job, work, retire and watch my kids follow the same process". Man, what a load of bullshit! That's what you're basically force-fed of what is 'supposed' to happen. It doesn't have to be.

Do whatever it is that makes you happy. Grind your ass off, but enjoy it. Blaze your own trail, but enjoy the ride of it and with those who are around you. There is no template. You create the map.

The only other thing I can tell you is to always put something back. It's great when you're making money, but always remember to save some. The smartest thing you can do is set up something where a percentage of what you make automatically goes into investments. This way, you can budget what you have coming in and you can save a good chunk at the same time. If you're used to making

$5,000 a month and you start making $15,000 a month, take $6,000 a month and stock it away. Act like you never even made it! Just set it and have it automatically go into investments and you'll build yourself a nice stock pile in no time.

Finally, and my personal favorite, never forget who you are or where you came from. When you've reached the things you've been striving for, and you *will* reach them, look for ways to give back. Remember what it was like when you first started this journey.

Remember how it felt to be striving, grinding and climbing the food chain. Recognize those who are now grinding, just as you did, and lend a hand. You'll be able to tell which of them "have it" and which ones are pretending. Help those who are doing it. It's the right thing to do.

It doesn't matter if you believe it or not, karma's real. You can bet everything you have that if you give it the opportunity, it's going to bite you in the ass.

If you've made it this far, I must not have bored you enough to put the book down. So at this point, I'll congratulate you. You're well on your way!

There are two parts of this book left. The following chapters are more about me personally, and what led me to come up with this formula. You will gain some knowledge from some of it, and some of it is just me rambling about a few things.

The last part is an actual "walk you through it, step-by-step blueprint" on how to plan out your schedule as mentioned in the beginning chapters. If you'd like to skip the self-serving part about me and my personal story, just flip to page 131. If you want a little more insight into my thoughts and how it works, then turn the page.

Chapter 15

It's All About The Hustle

Everyone has to begin somewhere, so I will take you back to when it began for me. If I think about it, it really started for me when I was in the ninth grade. I didn't call it a business then, but looking back now that's exactly what it was. It is a funny story actually, because I was almost like a bookie. Of course, I didn't realize I was doing anything illegal, but it was very close to how that word is defined.

I've always loved football and back then I would study up on all of the college and professional games. I knew who the good teams and players were, and I knew which players had injuries or off-the-field issues. I would look at how many road games in a row they'd played and how far they had traveled in between them. Having this information gave me an advantage over the game and I began taking bets on who was going to win. It was a simple model. If you won, I would pay you and if you lost, you would pay me. I didn't even know or understand point spreads at the time, so there wasn't any "You bet fifty dollars and I'll pay you thirty dollars" kind of thing. It was straight up simple, and I liked it.

Everybody was into football, so I just found a way to make money on it. I thought to myself "Hey nobody's doing this, I'll try this." I printed out sheets and handed them to everyone I came across. The sheets came with simple instructions and an opportunity to make some money. I'd tell them "You can pick five games. Circle the ones you want and how much you want to bet on each game." Every week would bring in fifteen to twenty people who were in the game and they had a good time, and I was making money. During the football season, I was busy and when the season was over I found other ways to make money.

Looking back now, I can say I always liked the idea of a good game with odds. Gambling is something competitive to do and I was good at it. Even to this day, I'll pretty much bet on anything, if I know anything about it.

My school at the time was in Jacksonville, Alabama, on the Jax State Campus. It was cool to have the high school be located on a college campus, but what was even better was the fact I made money because of it. Back then we had the freedom to roam around the school as we pleased. This was before every school had police and "boundaries". Hell, you could still go home for lunch at the time and as long as you were back by class time, nobody cared.

The commerce building where the college sold food, drinks and books also had one isle that was filled with candy. I remember thinking "the high school kids would be here all day long." In fact, I began to wonder how come I was the only one (or one of the few) who walked over here at all. But when I realized that no one else was coming, another idea was born.

I would take my lunch money and go there at the start of lunch or in between classes. I would buy a load of candy and I'd bring it by the school and sell it. Yeah, the other kids could have walked over for their candy, or even planned ahead and brought candy from home. But they didn't. In the isles, when the munchies hit them, I was there with the candy, ready to sell and make a profit. I would buy the candy bars for ten cents apiece and I would sell them for a quarter each in the halls and by the lockers.

I was fascinated that I could make money so easily by charging more than double for the candy I bought just minutes before a short walk away. Honestly I didn't really care why they wouldn't just go get it themselves, I was happy to make the trip. I always sold out and I took the profits and reinvested it into more candy. It was around that time I realized how lazy most people really are.

For a thirteen year old kid, I was making pretty good money selling candy. That is, until the teachers found out and made me stop. Damn those teachers, trying to stunt the beginning entrepreneurial workings of a guy with a plan (and business)!

Of course from that point, they kept a close eye on me in the classes and hallways. So what do you do when a challenge appears? You don't focus on the problem, you focus on the solution. I wasn't worried about getting in trouble, I wasn't doing anything illegal. I was more focused on finding a place I could sell the candy!

It took me all of about twenty minutes to set up sales in the parking lot. Right back in business!

Back then we'd all keep our books or backpacks in the car and run to the parking lot between classes. It was a way to step out of that school environment and regroup, even if for a moment. What better way to go back to class then with a nice sugar rush from a candy bar. The teachers actually helped me improve the business because the parking lot was a much more profitable location. So to Mrs. Miller and others, thank you! I probably earned as much as you did those years. I learned to adapt early.

It didn't occur to me that what I was doing was an actual business. I was just smiling because I was making some money on a few creative ideas. Inherently, I believe that all kids are creative. If you give them the chance to experiment they'll learn to look for solutions to common problems. Being allowed to monetize or profit on the solutions they provide, kids would learn entrepreneurship and business completely on their own.

I never liked sitting in school. I went because I had to. It came too easy. I was bored and it just took too much out of the day. If you talked to my mom, to this day she's still rather angry with me about the way I handled school. I would get A's and B's, but I never cracked a textbook. Most of what they taught was common sense and once you have the basics, what else do you really need in life?

Sometimes I would just roll into class and know it. I don't know how I knew it, but I did. Maybe it's because I was interested in the world around me. I always asked a lot of questions. I wanted to know how things worked and why they were the way they were. I was fascinated with history and by getting all of that information on my own, by the time we started to talk about it in school, I was already on to the next thing.

When I said I never cracked a textbook, I meant it. But as far as reading other books, I loved to read. I still do.

If something interests me, I want to go as deep as I can in the subject, and once I'm in, I'll retain it.

The only subject I had difficulty with in school was math. I never cared to learn it, honestly. I remember wondering when the hell I would ever put algebra and calculus into actual practice. To this day I never have because they have calculators for that shit!

As long as I could plan, count my profits, balance my gross and net against expenses, then that was enough for me. The rest could be handled by a calculator, or better, a qualified accountant who loves the numbers game. I knew that I was never going to build a highway, a bridge or a skyscraper, so geometry was nonsense that meant nothing to me. I took it because I had to. See Mrs. Wingo, no matter how much you tried to break my balls, I told you I'd never need it. I was RIGHT and I find it hilarious!

The hustle started early for me. I learned very early that if you make it easy for people to get what they want, they'll pay you for it. The football and candy store was just the beginning. I took the hustle to a whole other level just a couple short years later.

Chapter 16

Here's A Couple Tee's To Stick Them On

I started playing golf at around the age of fourteen and quickly became obsessed. All I wanted to do was play. The school bus used to go right by the course I played at, and I would just have them drop me off there. From the moment I was out of school, you could find me on the golf course. Little did I know that the candy selling business was pocket change compared to what you could make on the golf course!

It took me about a year to get good enough to be able to hold my own with the better players. Kindly enough, my dad and his friends let me play with them while I was developing my game. Of course, they had no problem taking my money either! We never played for much, but there were more than few times I list ten dollars or so.

Slowly I started to get closer and closer to their level and the money I lost would sometimes turn into me winning. It wasn't long after that I was taking their money just about every time we played. What amused me more than anything was while they had no problem taking my money for a good year, a month or two after I started taking theirs, they didn't want me playing with them anymore!

Of course, I didn't find this out till years later when my dad told me. He never stopped playing me for money though, I just had to give him strokes.

What I started to notice was the better players always had some sort of game going. While I didn't really know any of them personally, they had seen me around the course often enough that they would smile and say "hello". One day I got up the nerve to ask them if I could play in their game. I honestly didn't expect them to say "yes", but hey, if you never ask, you never know!

It was there that I realized how good I had become. I was more than able to hold my own with them and I often beat a good number of them. Instead of playing for quarters, we started playing for twenty dollars or more. Here's the fun part. Being a fourteen year old kid, I realized very quickly that most anyone I met that was older, never really thought I had a chance to beat them. This belief cost a lot of people a lot of money!

Whoa! There is that ego thing, getting in the way again! This was before *Tiger Woods* came along and let everyone know you can't underestimate younger people. I was just a punk kid to these people and there was no way they would admit to themselves they couldn't beat me. This mistake cost people their clubs, dinners, balls, bags and anything else I could think of, to barter with.

The first time I came home with someone else's driver, my dad looked at me like I had stolen it. He couldn't really believe I had played someone for their club. That meant I had to put mine up too, and if I had lost, I would have had to give them mine.

It happened so many times he just began to laugh.

As I got deeper into the sport, I began to realize how expensive a lot of the equipment was. I didn't have a job and I wasn't selling candy anymore, so I didn't really have any money. My dad would buy me golf balls at times, but most times I would find them in the woods. I quickly began to realize that in all of the lakes around the course, there were golf balls that people had mis-hit into them.

I knew how much people were paying for balls by what the pro shop was selling them for. I would just sell mine for a little lower and make some money. Okay, I made more than 'some money', I made hundreds!

A friend and I would get into these lakes after dark, and get thousands of balls out of them. We got so many one time we broke a wheelbarrow and had to call my dad to come pick us up. We'd soak them in water and bleach for twenty-four hours or so and then sell them right on the first tee box.

I have never seen anyone get away with that on a golf course. Usually the pro there will make you stop it immediately because you're taking money away from their shop. For some reason, they let me do it. I made upwards of three hundred dollars on my best days and there were always people hitting these balls back into the water! I would run out and then just go and get more.

It's pretty crazy to look back at it now, but I figured out multiple ways to make money from the game I loved to play. I'd gamble, sell golf balls and help them marshal so I didn't have to pay for practice. Obviously, back then I never really looked at it like I was building a business, I was just a kid who figured out a crafty way to make money. I recognize it now, but back then I was just happy not to have to ask my parents for money. I'm sure they were happy about it, too!

Chapter 17

School? Please....

The only thing I liked about school was the people that I met while I was there. I got good grades, but honestly, the only reason I gave a shit was my parents would kick me off whatever sports team I was playing if got below a 'B' and that only happened twice. I loved competition and sports was where I got it, so to have that taken away from me was more than enough motivation to keep my grades up.

College, though, was a whole other story. I was eighteen years old and the fear of having anything taken away from me was gone. I'll admit that the last year I was living at home was a rough one for both my parents and myself. I had my mind set on doing things how I wanted to do them, and of course, they had their minds set on how I was going to do them.

The day I graduated, I pretty much packed my shit and left. One of the few things I've done that I regret was not taking one of a couple golf scholarships. Looking back on it now, I can't say things turned out bad because of it, I've done extremely well. But I look back on it now and wish I had taken one of them. I enrolled in a local university about ten minutes down the road from my parents' house.

I had played golf with their golf team many times, so I knew most of the guys on the team. I knew I could beat half of them, so there was no question I was making the team. What I wasn't ready for was the worthless coach that ran the team. He wasn't even a coach really, he was the school's athletic director and just took on the golf team as a hobby.

When you talk about college sports, you would figure they would have some sort of structure to their program. At least that's what I was expecting from it. What I got instead was a waste of time from a coach who didn't know his head from his ass. Our practice consisted of playing a round and turning our score cards in when we were done. I had more structure in high school and I let it be known.

Obviously, the coach didn't like this. "Who is this punk kid coming in here and bashing the way I run my team?" That's the thing though, you never know if things will change until you bring it to someone's attention, and you can't just go through life accepting things as if that's just the way they are. Question everything you think isn't right, no matter what the authority figure says. I still do it every chance I get.

Needless to say, this coach and I weren't on the best of terms. One morning, he called my dorm room at 6:30 a.m. and I didn't have class until 10:00 a.m. There was no way I was waking up that early, so I was pretty pissed off that my phone was going off. I rolled over, grabbed the phone and answered it with "Someone had better be in bad shape to be calling me this fucking early". Those were the last few seconds of my college golf career. After that conversation, there was no way I was playing for this jack ass.

With golf gone, I had no more interest in being in school. I had just done twelve years of school and I figured out real quick that first two years in college were nothing but the same crap I had already done. Why is that anyway? It seems to me that more people would actually finish college, or maybe even give a shit, if they could go right into figuring out what it is they want to do!

It would make much more sense to take the first year and test out a few different work programs to see which profession you want to go into. The moment you decide, then you start taking the courses you need to graduate with that degree. Too many people just go in and get some general bullshit degree that does absolutely nothing for them. Honestly, what are you going to do with a degree in "business"?

The first thing I did was look to figure out how I could make some money. I had a job waiting tables a couple of nights a week, but that didn't pay much. Once again I found an angle and I exploited the hell out of it. Anyone who's been to college knows there's a lot of drinking going on. If they're paying attention, they also realize that it's rare that anyone plans for the after party! So what did I do? I started delivering beer to people and getting paid for it.

The key to most things is to find something people are already doing and then go about making it easier for them to do. If you do that, they'll gladly pay your for it. They were already drinking, I just made it so they didn't have to go out and get their drinks in the middle of their party. People loved it and I was as busy as I wanted to be. When I made enough for the night, I'd stop taking phone calls.

Supply and demand. It's the foundation of all business.

I was enrolled for a year, but I really only went for about two weeks. I basically ran my beer run business while living in the dorm room. I was smart enough to withdraw from every class I had so it wouldn't hurt my GPA if I ever wanted to go back, but I never have. It was pretty interesting explaining that to my parents, though. They weren't very happy, to say the least!

From that point is where I joined a fraternity and wasted a good year. Well, I can't say it was wasted. I had a damn good time! But that year wasn't the most productive, to say the least. Unless you can count success by how many beers you drank!

This is also where the "moment" I talked about in the early part of this book happened and I knew I had to get out. I packed my stuff and I moved to Florida in 1997 to play professional golf.

Chapter 18

The FBI Shuts It Down

I'll fast forward through my years of bartending and waiting tables while I was playing golf in Florida. That is a whole other book in itself. If I ever do write it, I bet the amount of people who go out to eat at restaurants will drastically decrease. I'll just leave it at that.

While I may own a company that has processed seventy plus million dollars online, in 2008 I had never even sent an email. Honestly, I didn't want anything to do with computers. I thought they were for lazy people who just didn't want to pick up the phone or get a real job. I felt the same way about cell phones. I thought they were electronic leashes, and if you didn't know where I was, there was a reason for it. Oh, how times have changed.

Having stopped playing golf at this point, I was working twelve to fourteen hour days in construction. My uncle just happened to be coming down to Florida for a convention that had to do with a company he had got involved with. He really didn't want to tell me what it was, or how it worked, but I kept pestering him until he gave in. Little did I know, within the next two months I'd be dealing with the FBI, the loss of five thousand dollars and the birth of my online career! To be clear, NONE of what happened was my uncle's fault. He lost money, just like I did.

Seeing that I knew nothing about how the internet worked, when he told me he was getting paid for just viewing websites for a number of seconds, I wanted in. The way it worked was that you bought what they called "ad packs". You had to put in your own website to advertise, and other people would view it and you would make sales. Of course, nobody ever bought anything because they were all just viewing websites so they could get paid. Basically, it was a form of a traffic exchange. Back then, I had no idea what it was, I just thought it was great that I was going to get paid for looking at websites for thirty seconds each.

The convention had a special deal that whatever dollar amount you put in, they would double in ad packs for you. My uncle was doing pretty well with it so I took out five thousand dollars and asked him put it in for me. This let me start out with ten thousand ad packs.

Each day I had to view ten websites for thirty seconds each, and as long as I did that, I got a "credit" on my account. As the credits grew, I could turn them into money and then cash out. I did this for almost two months and was just days away from making my first withdrawal when it all came crashing down.

I went to log in to the site to view my daily sites and instead of hitting the welcome page, I got a page with a big FBI logo on it saying they had seized the site. Now, not knowing anything about the internet other than viewing these websites, I was pretty freaked out! I thought maybe I had logged in the wrong place or it was some kind of mistake. I tried it about twenty more times, and each time that big FBI logo was looking back at me. I finally called my uncle to see if he had the same thing happening to him, and he did.

It stayed like that for months and I finally just had to accept the fact I wasn't getting my money back.

This, of course, pissed me off! The five grand didn't take food off my plate, but that's not a small amount of money. I wanted it back and be damned if I wasn't going to get it! I did what most people do at some point, I went to *Google* and typed in "how to make money online".

I was hooked in the first thirty seconds. I read sales pages, and crazy wild claims. There were people swearing that they were making millions while sitting on the beach. I saw it all and I wanted to buy as many things as I could. I went looking for reviews for things and, of course, they were all positive for everything I looked at. I was so green at the time it wasn't even funny. I had no idea about affiliates or people doing review sites. I was the perfect online customer, completely oblivious to it all!

The first program I bought was something called *The Rich Jerk*. I still think it's a funny product, especially the way the sales video was done. There is a smart ass Italian guy flat out telling you he's richer than you'll ever be, that he has more things, he makes more money and he's insulting you in every way you can think of. It was great!

It was there that I learned about review sites and how everything I had read as far as reviews were nothing more than affiliates using a creative way to make a commission. I also realized that reading a real review of something online was going to be a difficult thing to do. Even then, I was looking at things differently. Instead of saying "Yeah, I'm going to build some sites like that and make some money...", I looked at it as "Okay, from this point on you can't believe anything you read as far as reviews go".

As I was digging around, I came across a very popular marketing forum that looked to be full of information. I spent weeks reading everything I could. There were opinions, arguments, product reviews (real ones) and more. I had found what I was looking for, and I knew it was time to put the system I explained in the thirteen steps in this book into play.

The first experience I had was horrible. I signed up for a guy's course where he was supposed to show us how to make a hundred dollars a day just by following him. He would do a video on what he was doing to the site he was building and then post it in the membership area each day. This lasted about two weeks and then he just disappeared. This obviously pissed a lot of people off, but unlike most, instead of bitching about it, I went back over what he had shown in those two weeks and pulled all that I could learn from it.

For getting the basics down, he did a pretty good job. He just wasn't as good as he thought he was, and he couldn't complete the promise he had made when sold it to us. I started to look for something else very similar to what he was teaching, or a course where it was a "watch me do it" course. Luckily, I found it, along with two people who changed everything for me.

These guys used the first guys' failure to not only drag all of us into their course, but a whole shit load of others as well. Within the first four days they were making money and they were doing the same things at the start that the first guy was doing. I was following along and doing the things they showed, but I wasn't getting the same results they were. After a week or two of this I put the "old faithful" tactic of just asking them a ton of questions. Looking back on it now, I was probably a pain in the ass, but hey, I wanted to succeed and if that's what I had to do, I was going to do it.

Finally one day, after asking them a shitload of questions, one of them just gave me their phone number and told me to call him. While on the phone with him, I made sure to let him know I wasn't wasting his time and that I wouldn't bug him on the phone. He was really cool about the whole thing. He told me if he didn't want to hear from me he wouldn't have given me his number, and to use it whenever I needed to.

Here you have an example of what I talked about earlier when I said to give back, to help others. These guys were doing just that, and I appreciated it. I had also just aligned myself with those who were doing better than I was and as long as I stayed in that circle, my marketing would go up. Did it ever!

Before long, they weren't just teaching me. They were showing me things and I was showing them things and it was more of a mutual friendship. I started this whole process in August and I made my first sale in October. By the time November came around, I was making more money in just a few hours a day (although they were the hours of 11:00 p.m. to 3:00 a.m.) than I was working fourteen hour days in construction.

To this day, I am still grateful to those guys for the time they spent with me. They're not partners anymore, and one of them I haven't talked to in years, but I'd still give either one of them the shirt off my back if they asked for it. I wrote earlier about never forgetting where you come from and even though I've had great success, I still remember that feeling when they told me to call them. I've done this numerous times for others just as a way to pay it back. I really believe that kind of stuff is important. It is a part of your character and who you are.

Don't get it mixed up though! They didn't hand me anything and they surely didn't give away any "secrets' until I was able to start showing them some things I had picked up. They made damn sure I was putting in the work before they got comfortable enough with me to treat me as someone on their level.

I bring that part of it up to show you that I started at the very bottom and worked my way to the top. Nobody is going to hand you anything, but if they see you're busting your ass, they're much more willing to help you out. Many of them remember what it's like to be there and they can respect someone who is grinding just as they did.

Chapter 19

Enjoy The Ride

I could go on and on about all the things I went through to get to where I am today, but I think I've done enough of that. I've given you everything I used, both mentally and physically, to achieve it. I've given you different ways to think and look at things. It's not always black and white. There are certainly things those shades of grey keep covered. But if you look hard enough, you'll see them in full color.

Honestly, I've been more successful than I ever thought I'd be at this point in my life. I always knew I'd get there at some point, but I never thought it would be this fast. When I finally took a good hard look at all the things, situations and positions I've been in, it hit me. I had done the exact same thing in every situation where I had success. The more I analyzed it, the more it began to stick out. It stuck out so much, it's like everything else just faded away.

I know without a doubt that you could take everything away from me and within a short amount of time I could get it all back. You could stick me in pretty much any situation you wanted to, and I could come out on top. I'm not saying that to be egotistical or cocky, I truly believe it and I've proven it.

The older I've gotten, the faster time goes. My oldest daughter is almost nine now and I can remember her being born like it was yesterday. My twin daughters are almost five and I can remember the day they were born like it was yesterday. Hell, I can remember turning twenty and twenty-one in the same bar and that was almost twenty years ago! As kids we were always told it would go faster as we got older. Holy shit, is that the truth!

The thing I'm most proud of is that the money and the success have not changed me as a person. Sure, I have a fancy car and a nice house. May as well have some fun with some of the money! You can't take it with you when you go, right?

But I still have the same friends since the day I started this venture. I still enjoy going to a good dive bar and shooting pool over going to a fancy club and sitting at the VIP tables. I get a kick out of going to buy a fancy car dressed like a bum. If I go somewhere, I want to meet and have a drink with everybody there just because I like people. I like the people who give back. Those who don't look down on people because they have more, or are more popular.

What can I say, I have a little back woods country in me still, no matter how much being an Army brat tried to take it out of me. You won't ever catch me in a suit unless I'm at a wedding, or in court, and you will be lucky to see me without a hat on. It just is what it is.

At the end of the day, as long as you're still breathing, everything else is temporary. You can turn the next moment into whatever you want it to be, it's all up to you.

I don't know who came up with this phrase, but it's probably my favorite.

"Right now, this very moment, is the oldest you've ever been and the youngest you'll ever be again, don't waste it."

Those are words to live and prosper by.

The last part of this book is what I call *The Mindset Blueprint*. It will actually walk you through some of the steps I covered in the first chapters, but in greater detail. This last section alone has been responsible for many people's success and rejuvenation.

I thank you for spending some time with me through this book. I hope you take what I have shared and use it to take you to whatever level you want. More than that though, I hope to meet you some day and hear your story over a beer or two. Be safe and be well. Be a good person, be a good friend and be a good leader. Work hard and change something. Change someone and better someone's life.

If I have met you, well, you owe me a beer and I'll see you at the bar!

P.S. I didn't create these things on the following page and I don't know who did it first, so I can't give proper credit. I just like the mentality behind them and I want to share them with you.

Take them as you will…

The Top 18 Principles of Successful People

1. Unsuccessful people think everything is too good to be true. Successful people think that getting a job sounds too bad to be true.

2. Unsuccessful people give up when things don't go their way; a few disappointments and they are onto something else, saying things like "It wasn't hard for me". The successful work harder and become more determined when things go bad, and understand that you have to take the bad with the good to make it.

3. Unsuccessful people always have an excuse. Successful people say "my fault" and they refuse to make excuses.

4. Unsuccessful people think that not getting what they want is okay. Successful people are disgusted at the thought of not getting what they want, and they will do whatever it takes.

5. Unsuccessful people always have to talk it over with their unsuccessful friends to make sure no one will make fun of them if they make a decision. Successful people think for themselves and couldn't care less what their friends think.

6. Unsuccessful people are never coachable or teachable. Successful people are always learning, even when the money starts coming in. They never stop learning from those who were there first.

7. Unsuccessful people are scared of others. Successful people entrust in others and know that other people are crucial for their success.

8. Unsuccessful people are always procrastinating; they would rather talk about it, read about it, think about it, but never seem to *do* anything about it. Successful people hate doing anything but getting it done.

9. Unsuccessful people are glad when the day is over. Successful people love when the day begins.

10. Unsuccessful people think successful people are lucky. Successful people put themselves into a position to be "lucky", and then work hard to make the "luck" show up.

11. Unsuccessful people work by the hour. Successful people work by the month. Unsuccessful people want to know that after one hour of work they have something to show for it. Successful people find unsuccessful people who think like that and make them their employees.

12. Unsuccessful people get excited they just got hired. Successful people think it is funny that someone could be fooled that easily; they are just making the successful person more successful (and rich!).

13. Unsuccessful people complain a lot. Successful people are thankful that no one shot at them today, that they didn't have to fight in a war, and that they

don't have a job.

14. Unsuccessful people are too concerned about what other people are doing. Successful people are only concerned about what they can be doing to get more done.

15. Unsuccessful people think that if no one is doing something, it must suck. Successful people think that if no one is doing something, it means more money for them.

16. Unsuccessful people think that if everyone (all two hundred people at the meeting in a city of one million) is doing something, it must be saturated. Successful people think that unsuccessful people aren't too bright.

17. Unsuccessful people think it is okay for other people to live where they want to live, drive what they want to drive, and do what they want to do. Unsuccessful people are okay with the fact that they can't do these things. Successful people get sick just thinking about being average.

18. Unsuccessful people think that other people's opinions are worth more than their dreams. Successful people know that their dreams are worth more than other people's opinions.

"To be successful, you must learn from the unsuccessful and do not do what they do nor think how they think."

Chapter 20

The Fastest Way To Becoming A Productive Machine

The Mindset Blueprint is something I wrote a long time ago, but everything in it is just as powerful today as it was then. This short report is responsible for turning around many people's businesses and work ethic because it forces you to be productive. If you follow it, it's impossible not to be.

As I mentioned in the first couple chapters at the beginning of this book, I still follow the blueprint to this day. There will be parts in here that are in some of the chapters, but I also wanted to put it in this book in its entirety. It's sort of a quick start guide, but ten times more powerful when combined with the steps! It's written toward the person attempting to make a living by doing things online, but it can be applied to anything.

Use it, do it and profit from it.

The Mindset Blueprint

When I first got started online there was nothing but distractions! I'm sure you can relate, but what I'm about to show you is not only going to teach you how to deal with these distractions, I'm going to show you how to make them a positive force!

By following what you're about to learn, the changes to your business and to your life will be tremendous.

You see, the one thing that separates people who are successful is having the ability to block out all the distractions and focus on **PRODUCTIVE** tasks. They don't let things distract them, but at the same time they're don't spend their entire lives with their nose to the grind stone, either. They know exactly what they need to do and how they need to do it to get there. You're going to be shown how to do this in this blueprint. By doing these things, you avoid all of the things that basically do nothing more than waste a huge portion of your day, and it will force you to turn the corner in your business.

You may be thinking that you are not one of these people, but I'm going to show you a way here that will prove to you that you waste a lot more time during the day than you think. I didn't think I was one of the "time wasters" myself at one point, but once I did this exercise, I was completely floored by what I found out. Yep, I was a time waster, too!

Another thing I see that causes people lot of problems are the way they set their goals. We hear so much about how you should set goals, and this is true, but has anyone ever taught you a way to set goals that are achievable?

All goals are achievable, but what I mean is setting goals in a very specific manner that allows them to build on top of each other to reach the major ones. There is a HUGE difference and it is a vital part of a person's success. Setting your goals the wrong way will kill your business.

By the time you finish reading this, if you apply what is herein, I promise you that it will change your life.

Now, just reading it won't do it. You MUST put it into action! That is where the power of what you are about to learn comes in. You are going to change the way you do things completely from this day forward and if you do, you will be more productive than 99% of anyone who ever tried to make money online.

The truth is, this can be applied to ANYTHING you want to apply it to. I'm just using working online as an example, but this formula can be used for an offline business, relationships, homework, sports or any other thing you can possibly think of.

So, let's get you going and start putting the pieces together.

Part 1 – Your Plan

Every successful business starts with a plan. I don't care if it's a beauty salon, radio shop, service repair company, or an online business. Every single one that has been successful began with a plan. This is where a lot of people really screw up. I like to equate it someone trying to go on a diet.

Most people believe that when they start a diet, they have to rigidly stick to it or it's over. They soldier on for a good two weeks and never miss a workout or a meal. Then, all of a sudden life gets in the way and throws them a curve ball. They miss a couple workouts and they go right back to living like they are used to, thinking that they've totally screwed up and there's no point to continue with their plan. People look at plan like this too, and it's a sure way to assure that you fail.

There has never been anyone, anywhere that has ever laid out a plan and followed through with it to the 'T' without interruptions. It just doesn't work that way. But, it's those who have the ability to make adjustments for these interruptions that carry on and lose the weight in their diets and have success in their businesses.

So, the first thing is that you must have a plan, but I want you to consciously realize that your plan is just that. A Plan. It's not an "if I don't follow every single step on this plan to the 'T' then all of my hard work is for nothing."

To state the obvious, the reason we have a plan is:

- **You Have To Know Where You Are Going Before You Start**

- **If You Don't Have A Plan You Are Setting Yourself Up To Fail**

If you don't have a plan on where you are going, how do you expect to ever get anything right? The bottom line is, if you don't have a plan, you are setting yourself up to fail before you even get started.

If you have a plan, you have a 100% better chance of success than someone who does not!

What most people do is they will find out about something, read something and then dive right into it for a couple of weeks. Then they hear about or read something else, dive into that for a few weeks, forget what they were doing originally and then they hear about something else, and then dive into that, too. Sounds a lot like what people do in the *Internet Marketing* world doesn't it?

I want you to ask yourself right now, and be honest with your answer. How many products have you bought and followed the exact pattern in the above paragraph?

What happens is that people follow this pattern and they wind up wasting quite a few weeks, months and years following different things and then they wonder WHY they never get anywhere!

On top of this, when they are working on which ever 'flavor of the week' product they just bought, they aren't really being productive with how they're working it anyway. This is the exact pattern that 99% of people trying to make money online fall victim to.

If they had only sat down and figured out a plan of action. A course of action on how they were going to get to where they wanted to go, they would have been a lot more successful and wouldn't have been looking back on the last few months and wondering why they are no further along than when they started! So the first part of this is...

How Do You Create A Plan?

The truth is, you need to create two plans and this is the first place that most people really screw it up. This is the very beginning! If you screw up from the beginning, what do you think your chances are at success?

The two plans you are going to create are:

- **A Personal Plan**

- **A Business Plan**

Some people might look at that and wonder "Why do I need to create two plans? Can't I just make one plan and intertwine the two?"

The answer is no.

You are actually going to want to create your personal plan first. In fact, you don't want to even *think* about creating a business plan until AFTER you have created a personal plan.

The reason I say that you want to create a personal plan first verses creating your business plan is because your personal plan is made up of all of the things you want to do, all of the things you want to accomplish that you want your business to pay for!

Is that not why we work? To afford ourselves the luxuries that we want? We don't work because we like to punch a clock. We don't work because we like having to get up and go to the same place every single day, and we definitely don't work because we like being told what to do!

We work because we like the things that our work affords us and our families to have! If the things we wanted or needed didn't cost money then the truth is that most of us wouldn't work! We'd spend our days fishing, or out on the golf course. They certainly wouldn't be spent working. Not mine, anyway.

At one time or another, most of us have, or have had, a soul-sucking job where we go from 9:00 a.m. to 5:00 p.m. If your job is in construction, then the hours are more like from 6:00 a.m. to 7:00 p.m. and regardless of our time schedule, eventually, we reach the point where we have had enough. We want the lifestyle that allows us not to *have to* go to work today if we don't want to. We want to be able to just pick up and go somewhere if we want to and it is our own business that will afford us the ability to do just that. But these are the things that you want to have in your personal plan that you will then work your business plan around so you can achieve them!

So, what should your personal plan consist of?

Well, let me first tell you that I HIGHLY suggest that your personal plan be bigger than your business plan! These are your goals that YOU want for yourself, your family and those who are a part of your life. Is that not more important than what is on your business plan? I sure hope so!

So you want to make your personal plan bigger than your business plan. Put some time into this one too, and make it as emotional as you can.

Let's take a look at some examples…

Writing Your Personal Plan

Things You Want to Do With Your Family

Maybe you want to take your family to on a vacation to somewhere you have never been before. Maybe you want to be able to be at home with them for a couple of weeks and not do any work. Maybe you want to take the children to *Disney World* and not have to worry about the price it is going to cost you to get there. Maybe you want to be able to sit down and have a family dinner at a certain time every night with your family. I think we'd all agree that "family" time doesn't happen as much these days as it should. Hell, maybe you have always wanted to go visit Paris, Greece or anywhere outside of the place you live. These are all examples of things you want to put on your personal plan.

Since I live in Orlando, one of the things on my personal plan every year is to take the kids to *Disney World* three times a year. Even though I hate going, my kids love it, so I put it on my personal plan of things I want to do for them.

Things You Want To Do For Yourself

Some good examples of these things are quitting your day job, buying a new set of golf clubs, buying that fancy sports car you always wanted, paying off your house, getting the kids college tuition paid for ahead of time, getting season tickets to your favorite sports team, or working out at the gym at a certain time every day. These are all examples of things that should go on your personal plan because your business is going to afford you the ability to do them.

Where Do You Want To Be In Your Life

Examples of these would be things such as what age you want to stop working all together, where you want to live, and what you want to do with your time, be it fishing, golf, playing poker or whatever it is you love to do. It also includes having 'x' amount of money in the bank or set aside by the time you are 'x' age. These are all things that you should put on your personal plan.

Anything you want your business to pay for needs to go onto your personal plan!

The next step is important. You need to **WRITE ALL OF THESE THINGS DOWN** and you must **PUT A DATE** next to each one.

I want you to really take some time and think about what you want to put on your personal plan. This is YOUR LIFE we are talking about here, and you should take what you want very seriously. But the true power behind it is in writing these things down and putting a date next to each one of them. If you find yourself saying things like "Oh, I'll never be able to…" Then STOP IT RIGHT NOW! Just do it, no matter how silly you feel.

Just do it! Do it!

I don't care if the dates you put next to these things are one year from now or ten years down the road, but do it.

Each morning you wake up, I want you to read these goals on your personal plan before you go to work and I want you to read them **OUT LOUD**.

Your mind reacts to things much differently if you speak them and can hear them. If you simply read them in your head, you are giving your mind the ability to wander and the effectiveness is lost. When you read it out loud, you are forcing your mind to focus on the task at hand. The strongest 'magic' is happening in your subconscious when you say it out loud. While your mind is busy focusing on reading the words, your subconscious mind is the one paying attention and that's exactly what you want!

It doesn't matter if you are going to punch a clock or are already working from home, read them OUT LOUD every morning before you do anything else and then read them again before you go to sleep at night. Every morning, and every night.

You do this because you want to remind yourself each day what it is you are working towards. If you don't, you turn into a mindless zombie that just goes through each day like in the movie *Ground Hog Day*. Everything is the same, day in and day out.

You must know what you want and you must remind yourself what it is you want out of life every single day. The more you do this, the more your subconscious mind is trained and the more it begins to believe what it is being told. Again, that's when the real magic starts to happen.

This makes such a huge difference, I promise you. Trust me and commit to doing this every day and every night if you want to succeed.

I have my personal plan in my drawer right next to my alarm clock. The first thing I do every morning is open that drawer even before I get out of bed, and I read my personal plan out loud. My wife has gotten to the point where she can say it word for word just from hearing it so many times.

At first she thought it was funny, but when the money started coming in and she could shop a little more, she didn't find it so funny anymore. I'm going to tell you right now, when you see things on that plan that you have already accomplished, it is one hell of an awesome feeling.

So take some time right now and create your personal plan! Get as detailed as you can. Use locations, numbers, and dates. Seriously, stop reading this and go and do it right now and really put some thought and effort into this and then commit to reading it each and every day.

Once you have done that, now it's time to show you just how unproductive most people, including yourself really are without even realizing it.

Part 2 – How Productive Are You, Really?

Over the course of the last two years, I have met and talked with a lot of people who have tried to quit their jobs and work online. I've talked to a lot of other people who are just looking to make an extra hundred dollars or two, just to help out with the bills. For the most part, I've found one thing consistent with people who just can't seem to get it done and that is that they flat out don't *do* anything.

Now, I don't mean that as in they are sitting in front of their TV all day long and expecting money to come rolling into their accounts, but you'll see in a minute that they may as well have be because what they are doing isn't any better.

Here's how the usual conversation seems to go...

[them] "Hey Bryan, I just don't seem to be getting anywhere man. I'm putting in all this time and I'm just not getting any results."

[me] "Okay, well show me what you have done and I'll see if I can take a look at where you're getting messed up. What all have you done?"

[them] "Well, I've put out a couple articles and I've done a few back links. I've been working on this e-Book for a bit, but I only have about ten pages done, but I'm just not making any money so it's hard for me to stay motivated to keep going."

[me] "Okay, so how long have you been working on these things?"

[them] "It's been at least three weeks now and I'm at this computer like three hours a day."

Do you see the problem there?

You would be amazed at how many people I've spoken to where that the exact conversation has taken place. They swear they are sitting at their computer for three hours a day *working*, but all they have done is a couple articles and part of an e-book they have been working on for the last three weeks, which still is not even finished.

Here's the problem...

How much of those three hours per day do you think they have been working on productive tasks? I can tell you right now, it has more likely been maybe thirty minutes a day or even less. This is the exact trap that almost every single person who tries to make money online runs into.

Just by implementing these techniques in this report, I can get more done in a three hour time span than most people will get done in two weeks. I know it's scary, but that is how unproductive most people really are.

Here's what usually happens throughout the course of someone's "work day" online.

Out of a four hour period, most people only work for thirty minutes on productive tasks! That's a staggering amount of time to be lost when you think about it. If you do that for five days, you are really only working a total of two and a half hours out of twenty. Multiply that by a month and you worked a total of ten and a half hours for the *entire month*! That's less than two full eight hour days at a "punch the clock" job. How much do you really think you are going to get accomplished in those few hours a month? I mean, get real!

Yeah, you might be sitting in front of your computer for four whole hours, but that's not working! You will be surprised at how many people will SWEAR they are working when they are in front of their computer... I highly doubt it.
Here's what really happens...

The first thing most people do when they sit down at their computer is open up their email. I mean come on, somebody has had to have emailed you something right?

Depending on how many lists you are on and how many product launches are going on at the time, you can very easily spend thirty to forty-five minutes (or even more) just clicking on links in emails looking at all the "new flashy push button" stuff that has come out in the last twenty-four hours.

Then you look at your spam folder to make sure nothing "important" went there. At this point, you spend some more time deleting the old emails that you already read that you haven't deleted just yet.

You may be laughing, but it's not funny.

Maybe you got a few emails from friends talking about what happened this weekend or the game last night. Now, how many of you really only have one email account? So you repeat the process through the different email accounts that you have and before you know it, a precious hour (or more) is gone.

From there, most people will go jump over onto one of the forums to either see if there are any reviews on the products you have just gotten emails about, or maybe there was a thread that you were watching yesterday that you want to see if there have been any new replies to.

Many times you will find some kind of interesting topic that you notice as you're reading through that you'll now spend ten to fifteen minutes or so reading, including all of the replies.

Of course, once you finish reading that thread, you stop on

some flashy thread you stumbled upon that claims to show you how three-hundred and fifty thousand dollars was made in the last forty-eight hours, so of course, you have to read that, too. We all know it's hard to not do that on forums.

The above doesn't include the private messages that you might have been sent since yesterday, and of course, there are always more than one forum that most of us go to. The bottom line is that you have now just lost another forty-five minutes to an hour. So now, you've already lost almost two hours. That's almost half of your "work" time available to you, and it's gone! You can't get time back.

Now that you're finally off the forums and email, of course you need to go check up on your social media profiles. I mean, someone has to have sent you a friend request or posted on your wall on *Facebook*, right? We all like to think we're popular, so why wouldn't someone have sent you a request, right?

Of course, once you get there, you see the stories people are posting and spend a few minutes reading and replying to those, making sure to "Like" a few along the way. Then it's just natural that you head on over to *Twitter* too, to see what's going on over there. There is another thirty minutes to an hour of your work time, gone!

Oh wait, I can't leave out checking your *JVZoo* and *PayPal* accounts to see if you've made any money right? I mean, come on, with all this time you've been in front of the computer, someone has had to of bought something you are promoting, right?

So you spend about twenty minutes checking your money, hops, click through rates and percentages and every other thing that you can think of that has to do with your money. Of course, you most likely have more than just *JVZoo* and *PayPal* to look at too which means another twenty to thirty minutes is now gone!

Now, since it's been about three hours since you sat down, someone has had to of emailed you about something 'important', right? So back on over to the email accounts you go to check. But, on the way over there, someone sends you a message on *Skype* and you spend the next fifteen minutes or so chatting back and forth with them about whatever it is they *Skyped* you about.

NOW, that you've got all the important things you needed to do like checking emails, *Paypal* accounts, social media and *Skype* messages out of the way, now you can actually do some work, right?

So you spend the last thirty to forty-five minutes you have to "work" making a blog post, writing an article or working on that project you have been trying to finish up for the last two weeks.

Believe it or not, this is the exact blueprint of most people's day. But they will swear that they work four hours a day!
I'll say it again. Just because you sit down in front of your computer for four hours *does not* mean you are working!

If you are completely honest with yourself, you will admit that you find yourself in the group of those who follow this ritual daily.

I've been there myself. I've been in that group, and it is very easy to get caught up in that pattern of things. If you don't think this is you, then I want you to do this for the next week.

Are you ready?

For the next five days, I want you to write down *exactly* what you do and what times you are doing it while you are supposed to be working. I don't care if it's answering the phone, getting the mail or going to the bathroom. Write down anything that you do while you are on work time. Write down what you are doing, the time you start doing it and the time you stop doing it. Write down everything you do during your "work" time.

This means that if you get up to go to the bathroom at 3:00 p.m. and you get back at 3:05 p.m., write it down. If you start reading emails at 4:00 p.m., write it down. When you are done with your emails, write down the time you stopped. I don't care what you are doing, if you do something during the hours you have set aside to work, write it down for five consecutive days.

At the end of those five days, look over your daily sheets and see just how much time you have wasted on things that are NON PRODUCTIVE TASKS! I can assure you that for most of you reading this, it will be a staggering number of hours completely WASTED!

Now, are you ready for something that will blow your mind? It did mine when I first heard it, and the more and more that I looked at it, the more I found it to be the truth. I want you to read this next phrase a few times and let it sink in because once you realize the potential of it, it will literally blow your mind.

"If you work four PRODUCTIVE hours per day, for thirty-three days, you will have done more PRODUCTIVE WORK then 99% of the people trying to make money online will do in an ENTIRE YEAR"

Remember that most people only spend from two to two and a half hours a week on productive tasks. Multiply that by fifty-two weeks and you've only got one hundred and thirty hours per year. But if you work four hours per day on PRODUCTIVE tasks for ONE month and two days, you will have done more than most people will do in an ENTIRE YEAR!

Pretty crazy when you look at it like that isn't it? But it is true. Now imagine if you worked on productive tasks four hours a day, five days a week for an entire year? Your results would be absolutely huge!

Now do you see why the people who are successful get there? They don't spend their valuable time reading emails, reading forums, hanging around on social media, talking on *Skype* or reading sales letters DURING WORK TIME!

They schedule time in their day to do all of those things, but it's AFTER they have made sure that they have finished what they needed to finish for the day. Ask anyone who is successful and I promise you 99% of them will back that up. They are disciplined and focused on productive tasks and they let nothing distract them when they are working. Not the phone, not the kids, not *Skype*, not *Paypal*, none of it!

I want you to copy that paragraph in bold from the previous page down on a piece of paper and post it somewhere that you walk by every day. Stick it to your car steering wheel, your computer or even on your refrigerator. Once that sinks in, you will be amazed at how powerful that one powerful sentence will make you.

Pin-pointing these roadblocks in your work time is a huge part of retraining your work schedule. It's also a huge step to your success. It's okay to play around on *Skype* and all the other things that you like to waste time with, but make sure you do those AFTER you are done working first.

So now that you know what roadblocks we all put in our own way, how do you get around them? This is where your business plan comes in.

Part 3 – Writing Your Business Plan

The first thing you need to understand when writing your business plan is that you MUST treat this as a business and NOT a hobby. If you treat this like a hobby, that is all it is ever going to be for you. Remember the things you wrote in your personal plan? Now ask yourself if those things are just a hobby for you.

The biggest mistake I see people make when they write out a business plan is that they write up these huge lofty goals but they have absolutely no direction on how they are going to get themselves there. This is a huge recipe for disaster!

When you set up your business plan the right way, this is extremely, extremely, extremely powerful! Yes, I wrote extremely three times because it really *is* that powerful.

For your business plan, I suggest you have all of these things included in it:

- **One Major Goal for the Year**

- **A Four Quarter Break Down**

- **A Three Month Goal**

- **A One Month Goal**

Your major goal for the year can be anything financial or "product" related. So if you want to make one hundred thousand dollars this year, then that could be a part of your *Major Goal for the Year*. If you want to make one hundred thousand dollars for the year and you want to have created ten products for the year, then that is your *Major Goal for the Year.*

Now this is just an example, because each of us will have something different here, but look back at your personal goals and base your *Major Goal for the Year* or other business goals off of that.

So, let's just say that you have chosen that you want to make one hundred thousand dollars for this coming year. Under that *Major Goal for the Year*, this is where you would use the *Four Quarter Break Down* on how you are going to get there.

So let's say you want to get to that mark by creating ten products this year and each one of them will need to sell ten thousand dollars' worth of copies to get there.

So since you have twelve months in the year, you will need to basically put out one product every month and quarter to get there. Now nobody go all math crazy on me, that's just a rough estimate! ;)

You now know that you are going to have to plan out how you are going to create those ten products, get them out there, and promote them in order to meet your major one year goal, right?

So now it's time to write up your *Three Month Goal*.

At month three, you should have basically have almost three products created and out there. This is where you are going to decide what products they are going to be, how many affiliates you want to have promoting, how many copies of them you want to have sold, and so on.

No major planning needs to be done here, you are just basically writing up an outline for what you want to have done by the end of month three. Nothing more than a small detailed *Three Month Goal*.

Now that you have that down, this is where you start to really dig in and create the plan that is going to propel you into the place you want to be, not only personally but financially, as well. So let's get in with a little more in detail with this one.

You are now going to set three *One Month Goals*. These goals are all going to lead up to having everything you set as your *Three Month Goal* completed. Months two and three don't have to be extremely detailed because we will be making changes to them, but the first *One Month Goal* MUST be detailed. It needs to be something like this example for this situation...

1. Have one project completed and fifty affiliates on board promoting by end of month.
2. End of week three, have thirty affiliates signed up and promoting.
3. End of week two, have split testing of sales page completed and fifteen affiliates.
4. End of week one, have product, website and affiliate program completed and testing begins.

Now, those are ONLY your goals. This is where it gets very powerful when you follow this system. You have your goals set up for the first month now, but how are you going to get there?

This is where you now take the FIRST week, which is number four on the list and you break it down into daily tasks to get it done. It needs to look something like this:

- Monday: Market research and product subject chosen.
- Tuesday: Product creation begins.
- Wednesday: Product creation finished and website design begins.
- Thursday: Website design finished and affiliate program installation begins.

- Friday: Affiliate program installation finished. Begin traffic generation to test sales page.

Now you have a very good outline of exactly what you need to do each day so you can accomplish your first weeks' goals of having your program totally up and running by the end of the first week. BUT, you're not done yet. That is a great start, but unless you are one of these people who is super focused, you can still waste a lot of time even with a good plan like that.

This is the most powerful part right here and something that MUST be done if you really want to have success! You now need to take each of those days and break them down into exact daily tasks for yourself to do each day. Not only do you need them broken down into daily tasks, you need to allow yourself times to do these tasks.

Let me state that these times are VERY important. These are WORK times and not goof-off times. During these times you need to tell everyone to LEAVE YOU ALONE!

Turn off your phone, turn off social media, email and *Skype*, and tell your wife or husband or whoever that if it is NOT an emergency, you are to be left alone. Tell them flat out you do not care what is going on. If it is not an emergency, you are not to be bothered.

I'm going to use a four hour work day as an example so, it would look like this:

Monday: Market research and product subject chosen.

1. 8:00 a.m. to 9:00 a.m., search hot topics on *Amazon, Google Trends, Facebook.*
2. 9:00 a.m. to 9:05 a.m., take a five minute break.
3. 9:05 a.m. to 10:05 a.m., look at other successful products in the same niche and write down your findings.
4. 10:05 a.m. to 10:10 a.m., take a five minute break.
5. 10:10 a.m. to 11:10 a.m., Compare sales pages of other products, read other products and compare likes and dislikes. How can I make my product better?
6. 11:10 a.m. to 11:15 a.m., take a five minute break.
7. 11:15 a.m. to 11:40 a.m., make a decision on what product to create.
8. 11:40 a.m. to 12:00 p.m., make plan for tomorrow.

Do you see what I have done there? I have given myself exact time frames to do each task that will allow me to reach the goal I have set for myself on the first day. You might be thinking "How do I know that the time I allow myself is going to be enough?"

Let me ask you this question. If someone put a gun to your head and told you that you have exactly one hour to research a topic and come back with some information on it, do you think you would do it?

Yeah, that's what I thought.

Don't allow yourself to over think it! Give yourself a time frame to do something and then STICK TO IT. If you've gone through your allotted time, then what you have is what you have! That's it. No excuses, no "Wait I need more time", none of that. You are on a schedule. You have a deadline and you MUST deliver. Period.

By doing it this way, you will slowly begin to realize just how effective you can be when you are working on a deadline like this. You will reprogram your brain to accept nothing less than what you demand be done. Set times and follow them. Many times you will be surprised by how much better the things you do are when you force yourself to work on a deadline. By doing this, you don't allow yourself to get distracted by anything else.

Another thing to notice is how I scheduled a five minute break after each task. Trust me, you NEED this break. I have found that you are most effective in one hour blocks when you are doing focused productive work like this. After an hour, your mind has a tendency to roam a little bit. This is the reason why I take a little five minute break after every hour I work.

I highly suggest you get up from your computer, go outside for a minute and get some fresh air. This allows yourself to relax a bit and refreshes your mind for the hour coming up.

I also want you to notice something VERY important that will ALWAYS be the last thing on your list for the day and that is to plan tomorrows work day out.

Now that you have finished the first day, you want to plan out the next day's daily tasks just like you did for Monday. I always put this as the last thing to do because just in case you had some sort of emergency during your day, you can always make adjustments.

Tuesday would look something like this:

Tuesday: Product creation begins.

9. 8:00 a.m. to 9:00 a.m., begin writing product. Table of contents and first two chapters are started.
10. 9:00 a.m. to 9:05 a.m., take a five minute break.
11. 9:05 a.m. to 10:05 a.m., second chapter is finished and third chapter is started.
12. 10:00 a.m. to 10:05 a.m., take a five minute break.
13. 10:10 a.m. to 11:10 a.m., third chapter is finished and fourth chapter is started.
14. 11:10 a.m. to 11:15 a.m., take a five minute break.
15. 11:15 a.m. to 11:40 a.m., fourth chapter is finished and all content is proofread for errors.
16. 11:40 a.m. to 12:00 p.m., make plan for tomorrow.

So again, you can see exactly what you are doing at the exact times during your work day.

Each task is written down so you can see exactly what you need to be doing at the time you should be doing it.

So now we have finished day two. Let's see what we would have planned for Wednesday.

Wednesday: Product creation finished and website design begins.

17. 8:00 a.m. to 9:00 a.m., fifth and sixth chapters started.

18. 9:00 a.m. to 9:05 a.m., take a five minute break.
19. 9:05 a.m. to 10:05 a.m., fifth and sixth chapters finished.
20. 10:05 a.m. to 10:10 a.m., tale a five minute break.
21. 10:10 a.m. to 11:10 a.m., final chapter started and graphics designer contacted.
22. 11:10 a.m. to 11:15 a.m., take a five minute break.
23. 11:15 a.m. to 11:40 a.m., product finished. Proofread and get design details sent.
24. 11:40 a.m. to 12:00 p.m., make plan for tomorrow.

Thursday: Website design finished and affiliate program installation begins.

25. 8:00 a.m. to 9:00 a.m., begin affiliate program installation, banners, emails, links.
26. 9:00 a.m. to 9:05 a.m., take a five minute break.
27. 9:05 a.m. to 10:05 a.m., review graphics and suggest changes. Begin sales page writing.
28. 10:05 a.m. to 10:10 a.m., take a five minute break.
29. 10:10 a.m. to 11:10 a.m., install website with graphics, continue sales page.
30. 11:10 a.m. to 11:15 a.m., take a five minute break.
31. 11:15 a.m. to 11:40 a.m., finish website, install affiliate program, banners, graphics, emails.
32. 11:40 a.m. to 12:00 p.m., make plan for tomorrow.

Friday: Affiliate program installation finished. Begin traffic generation to test sales page.

33. 8:00 a.m. to 9:00 a.m., continue with sales page.
34. 9:00 a.m. to 9:05 a.m., take a five minute break.
35. 9:05 a.m. to 10:05 a.m., continue with sales page.

36. 10:05 a.m. to 10:10 a.m., take a five minute break.
37. 10:10 a.m. to 11:10 a.m., double check everything to make sure it is all working properly.
38. 11:10 a.m. to 11:15 a.m., take a five minute break.
39. 11:15 a.m. to 11:40 a.m., begin testing sales conversions, email to list, articles, Facebook.
40. 11:40 a.m. to 12:00 p.m., make plan for tomorrow.

Now, what I've just done there is laid out an EXACT plan of action for someone creating a product on four hours a day in five days. From start to finish you have a plan.

For some people it may take a little longer, and for others it might be shorter because they will outsource more of it, BUT the bottom line is it's planned out in steps so you know exactly what you need to do each and every day.

If you do fall behind or something messes up your day, you ALWAYS have the "make plan for tomorrow" built in to your plan, so you can adjust tomorrows work accordingly.

What you have just done is created a plan to meet your week one goals and broken it down into smaller steps to make sure you get there. There is nothing mind blowing about, but what you have done is given yourself very small, very achievable goals each day that will allow you to meet your goal that you set for yourself for week one.

Now all you do is continue the pattern and do the exact same thing for weeks two, three and four, and by the end of the first month you will have met your *One Month Goal*. Then you just wash, rinse and repeat until you reach your second month goal, and so on down the road.

Here is how you get *in the zone* right as soon as you sit down to work. The night before, I want you to take your daily tasks for the day and stick them right on top of your keyboard. I don't want you to even be able to touch your computer until you see your daily task sheet. This is the easiest way to make sure that happens. Cover your keyboard with it and it will be the first thing you touch when you sit down, putting you right into work mode immediately.

I GUARANTEE you that if you follow this method of doing things you will be more productive than you have ever been and you will make more money than you ever have made. Once I started doing this, my income more than doubled in the first sixty days and I was doing alright before.

For some of you this may take making some major changes to the way you do things, but I promise you if you follow it, you will track me down in a month or two and thank me for it.

Setting goals is very powerful, but creating mini-plans of action, made up of smaller tasks that when combined allow you to reach those goals is a hundred times more powerful.

So, to recap this portion:

1. **Work in one hour blocks of time.**
2. **Take a five minute break after each hour.**
3. **Work with a timer to keep on plan.**
4. **Cut of all distractions.**

Number four on the above list is one that I want you to take very seriously. I know I wrote a lot about it earlier, but I want to drive home the point. When you are at a "punch the clock job" do you get personal phone calls? Does your spouse just come in and talk your ear off? Do your kids come in and want to sit on your lap? No, they don't because you would get in trouble.

If it continued, your work performance would suffer and your boss would probably fire your ass. So treat "work time" like work time and don't allow any of those things to distract or disturb you, just as you wouldn't be allowed to at a "real" job.

Follow that kind of a schedule.
Be that prepared.
Work that hard!

Your success is closer than you think!

About The Author

Bryan Zimmerman is a lifelong entrepreneur who from his early childhood has constantly tested the boundaries of conformity.

Always seeking a way to forge his own path and never accepting what is merely presented, he has achieved great success in multiple industries.

With his current company having processed over 70 Million dollars, Bryan is in high demand for consulting as well as speaking engagements.

Refusing to conform to what society deems a successful person should look like, what he enjoys most is blending in and meeting new people.

To book Bryan for consulting, or to speak at your next event, please call (407) 278-7179 or send an email with details to bryanzimerman@gmail.com.

Learn more about Bryan at:

www.BryanZimmermansBlog.com

Acknowledgments

Usually people put the acknowledgments in the front of a book, but I haven't done anything the way it's "supposed" to be done. So, in keeping with the same theme, I've saved the best for last.

First, let me just say I know I'm going to forget someone here and they're going to get upset about it. They may not ever tell me about it, they'll just hold onto it and let it fester. So I will just apologize now, in advance, and tell you it's not personal. There are so many people to thank and damn it, I'm only human. So if you think you should have been here and you're not, just know that I meant to put you here. Now get over it!

To the three teachers who I'd love to name here but I won't. You know who you are if you're reading this. Thank you for giving me the drive even at a young age to want to show you how wrong you were about me. I can see now that it wasn't me, it was your own disdain for your own lives that made you as negative as you were. I hope you got over it and learned how to be happy. You probably didn't though, so let me just say, it sucks to be you!

To Charlie King. Probably the best golf instructor I've ever run across. What I would have given to have you teach me when I was a kid. To this day you are still the most genuine person I know when it comes to how you treat people. I've seen you treat some people who will no doubt wind up in prison, the same way you treat a model citizen. You deserve all of the success and recognition that comes your way and I'm proud to call you a friend, even if you still haven't gotten me on *Augusta National*! Not to mention your son is named Bryan, so how can I not call you a genius!

To Phillip Welke. Thank you for the competition. You were the only one I've ever met who probably worked harder at your game than I did. You set a benchmark and it was fun and challenging competing with you. We haven't talked in twenty years and I have no idea what you're doing now, but maybe one day we'll run into each other again. I certainly haven't forgot you.

To all of my Pi Lamda Phi brothers from CNU. Holy shit, the stories I could tell but won't. You guys played such a huge role in my life for a short but awesome time. I wish I kept in touch with more of you than I have.

To Brian Tirch. Man, just let me apologize for being a total screw-up in keeping up with you. I am so bad at that and it's certainly not from you making the effort. Every time you come down this way something always happens and I can't get up with you. I remember how I used to yell at you to get off the damn computer and come out with us. How wrong was I back then? You're a great guy, have a great family and I should be a better friend and big brother. I'll get it right one of these days man, but don't think for a second I don't think about you often.

To Craig Bouchard, even though I've seen you once in the last ten years, you're still my best friend. I don't think I've ever had a friend where it was scary how much we thought a like. How the hell did we keep ourselves out of jail for all of those years? Lord knows we should have been there on more than a few occasions. No matter where you are man, I will always have your back. All you ever have to do is call.

To the other two Bouchard brothers. Never mind, I'm not going there. That might put me in jail yet!

To Cathy Sabofl. You are, without a doubt, the coolest boss I have ever worked for. You gave all of us the freedom to do and be as we were and that's rare. We all loved you for it. Don't think there's any doubt you know we would have done anything for you. You are a rare breed and more businesses would run successfully if owners treated people like you did. I hope you're doing well.

To Don and Jeremy. Even though you guys aren't partners in business anymore, I owe you guys more than I have to give. I will always be grateful for the time you spent with me when I first started out. It's rare, especially in this business, and without you two I don't know if I would have had the success I've had. I've made sure to pay that forward in hopes that those I've helped will do the same for others down the line. Thank you guys, I really mean that.

To my business partners, E. Brian Rose and Chad Casselman. Damn guys, what do I say? Nobody gave us a shot and more than a few called us crazy. We never doubted ourselves though, and once again that proves that's all that matters. We've fought like married people at times, partied like rock stars and everything in between. I know we've all changed each other's lives and the lives of others and I'm proud to not only call you guys business partners, but also friends. I look forward to what we do in the future.

To James, Kyle, Pierre, Justin and Chris. Playing music with you guys was one of the highlights of my life. We had a good time for those years! How many people can say they got to play at *Hard Rock* Live! I hope you're all doing well.

To Brad Gosse. Dude, what can I say here? Still one of only a few people I'll go to for advice on stuff. Even if it doesn't happen that often, I know you'll always be straight with me and not sugarcoat shit. Fire it up, man!

To Rymac. The *Dolphins* are STILL the only undefeated team in NFL history. Deal with it! You knew I was going to get that in there. Oh yeah, no safeties in pool when there is money on the table, that's just not cool. :)

To Brian Mitchel. It's good having you in the office and the radio with sports on all day keeps us both sane, I think! Keep grinding man, you'll get there!

To Jonathan Betancourt. You have no idea how much I'm looking forward to making you a household name in the tattoo industry. We're already off to an amazing start. Glad I met you, and even happier to be in business with you at *Realm Tattoos.*

To Nathan Green. How you deal with all the numbers and crazy shit we do is beyond me. It's been a pleasure to work with you sir, and the crew and I all thank you! Looking forward to working with you for years to come.

To Jeff and Joyce. How can I begin to thank you two? I don't know if there's enough room on these pages to even start. All I can say is "thank you". Thank you for all you have done, for all you have taught me and for just being there. If there is ever an example of those who would give you the shirt of their back if you needed, you two would be it.

To Rich. Man, how we didn't run into each other before we did is beyond me. I'd have to say I'm glad we didn't though, because if we did, there's no way you would have let me marry your sister! Of course, you wouldn't be married either! Thank God these cell phone cameras weren't around years ago or we'd both be in a world of trouble. Neither one of us will ever run for political office, that's for sure. You know if you ever need anything I'm right around the corner.

To my Mom. There's a million things I could thank you for, but the one that sticks out the most is teaching me to not just accept things. You always allowed us voice our opinion on things and that taught me to think beyond what's just in front of my face. There's no way to put a value on that. Thank you for always being there, for teaching me that no matter how I felt, the way I acted was going to have consequences I would have to deal with. That has kept me out of trouble more times than I can count. I love you!

To my Dad John. There is no way I can thank you for all the things you've done in my life. You never missed a game, you never tried to hold me back and you taught me if I wanted something bad enough, I would make it happen. You opened my eyes to things that many people dismiss as not possible. I hope I'm even half the dad that you didn't have to be. I love you!

To my Dad Gary. There's no doubt I get my love for music

and don't put up with people's shit mentality from you. It's served me well most times and it's taught me lessons other times. You taught me if a man can't keep his word, he's not worth a shit. That's something I take very seriously to this day. I wish we got to see each other more. You're still the only one I've seen hit a golf ball between your legs. I love you!

To my beautiful wife, Jen. I can't count the ways you've changed my life. When I was ready to leave the security of one thing to attempt something most people fail at, your confidence never wavered. I can't tell you how important that was then, and how you still continue to show that confidence in me in all my crazy business ventures now. You've been in my life longer than any other person I know and Lord knows you've seen every side of me there is. In a world where I'm used to people coming in and out of my life, you've been the rock. I thank you for that more than you know. Thank you for always believing and supporting me, even if you didn't understand it. I love you and I can't wait to see what the rest of our live brings us.

To my kids Ashley, Alyssa and Alexis. You're too young to read this now, but hopefully when you get older you'll see it. There was a time when the things I did were to benefit me. For the last nine years, even though sometimes it may not seem like it, everything I do is for you three. I hope you grow up believing that you can accomplish anything you put your minds to. Never let anyone hold you back. Chase your dreams, no matter how crazy people tell you they are. The only thing that truly matters in your life is that you're happy. Whatever it is that brings you that, do as much of it as you can. Be kind to those less fortunate than you, help people when you can, but above all else, love yourselves! There is only one you and don't ever let anyone try and change that. I love you all and no matter what you do in the years where you will hate me, I will always be there.

Finally, To Myself. Yes, I want to thank myself. Yeah, I know that's a weird thing to do, and it may even sound a bit egotistical, but the fact is I busted my ass to get where I am today. I'm proud of the things I've accomplished and the work I put in to get here. I laughed then and I laugh now when people tell me I can't do something. Maybe they just don't know me yet because if they did, they'd know better. My goal is to always climb the mountain and defend the peak of it. That may not sit well with people, but those are the same people who will worry more about the spelling errors or grammar mistakes in this book. My fondness for tattoos, hats, never wearing suits or anything else that doesn't measure up to what a successful person should be like. You'll learn very quickly that I don't do things how most "believe" they should be done. It may not be the way you'd do it, but that doesn't make my way the wrong way either. I live by my own code, and to me that's the only one that matters.

Other people I'd like to thank who have had an impact on my life in one form or another... Anyone who's ever used JVZoo, the rest of the Zoo Crew – Adam, Russell, John and Layne. Dennis, Brad Spencer, Mike Carraway, Rich Wilens, Siddique, Leah Butler Smith, Andrea Fulton, Valerie Duval, Abhi Dwivedi, Aiden Booth, Ali G, Andrew Fox, Anthony Aires, Ben Littlefield, Bertram Heath, Brian Johnson, Brian McLeod, Brian Prins, Chris Munch, Chuck Mullaney, Cindy Battye, Colin Theriot, Craig Bower, Damien Rufus, Darren

Monroe, David Eisner, Dennis Becker, Dennis Gaskill, Derek Pierce, Don Wilson, Dan Ardebilli, Ben Adkins, Dylan Kingsbury, Eric Oouviere, Gary Mahon, Gaz Cooper, Greg Rollett, Jeff Herschy, Jake Gray, Jason Fladlien, Jason Parker, Jeremy Gislason, Jeremy Schoemaker, Joe Troyer, Joel Comm, Jon Shugart, Jovana Sumar, Justin Popovic, Justin Wheeler, Kieth Dougherty, Kenster, Kevin Fahey, Kieran McDonogh, Lisa Gergets, Mario Brown, Mark Dulisse, Mark Helton, Mark Thompson, Martin O'Flynn, Martin Crumlish, Matt Garrett, Mick Kitor, Mike Cowles, Neil Napier, Pat Flanagan, Paul Clifford, Peter Garety, Precious Ngwu, Ricky Mataka, Robert Stukes, Roger Holmes, Ron Douglas, Ross Carrel, Russ Ruffino, Ryan Shaw, Sam England, Sam Bakker, Sean Kaye, Seth Beast Bias, Simon Greenhalgh, somon Hodgkinson, Simon Warner, Soren Jordansen, Stephen Renton, Tanner Larson, Tim Castleman, Tim Craggette, Travis Ketchum, Travis Petelle, Tommie Powers, Wah Bhatti, Walt Bayliss, WD Mino, William Meers, William Murray, William Twinner, Zed Shah, Gary Ambrose, John Cornetta, Kayla McDonald, Kris Dehnert, Mike Artime, Ezra Wyckoff, Jerome Johnson, Mathew Roe, Ross Goldberg, Peter Beattie, Mike Filsame Amber Jalink, Craig Crawford, Greig Wells, Alex Cass and finally

---

Insert your name above if I forgot you! :)

Special thanks to Kytka, Zynna and Zynnia!

www.ingramcontent.com/pod-product-compliance
Lightning Source LLC
Chambersburg PA
CBHW060559200326
41521CB00007B/618